Contents

Understanding Children's Learning

A Text for Teaching Assistants

Edited by Claire Alfrey

 David Fulton Publishers

This edition reprinted 2008 by Routledge
2 Park Square, Milton Park, Abingdon, Oxon, OX14 4RN
Simultaneously published in the USA and Canada
By Routledge
270 Madison Avenue, New York, NY 10016

First published 2003

10 9 8 7 6

The right of the individual contributors to be identified as the authors of
their work has been asserted by them in accordance with the Copyright,
Designs and Patents Act 1988.

British Library Cataloguing in Publication Data
A catalogue record for this book is available from the British Library.

ISBN 1 84312 069 0

Typeset by BookEns Ltd, Royston, Herts
Printed and bound in Great Britain

Acknowledgements

I would like to thank my colleagues who contributed to this book and helped me keep my sense of humour: the writers and James Arthur, Richard Bailey, Carl Parsons and Janet Tod, all of whom gave their time and support generously. I would also like to thank the Faculty of Education at Canterbury Christ Church University College who enabled me to develop alternative routes to gaining degrees and professional qualifications. In particular, I should like to thank all of our current Foundation Degree students and, especially, their predecessors on the Diploma of Higher Education, from whom we all learned a lot! Our work with these students has been both an inspiration and a privilege. They are a marvellous example of those coming into Higher Education from non-traditional academic backgrounds. Finally, I thank my family, Keith, Hugh, Angus and Margaret for all their time and patience.

Dedicated to the memory of Elma Little, someone who made everyone feel very special.

Notes on contributors

Claire Alfrey trained and taught in London. At Canterbury Christ Church University College she is Programme Director for the Graduate and Registered Teacher Programme and the Foundation Degree in Children and Young People Learning. Claire's specific interest over the past three years has been developing alternative routes into teaching, which includes the Foundation Degree as a way to obtaining a degree for teaching assistants who need to continue working. She has presented Canterbury Christ Church University College's developments for both the DfES and the Teacher Training Agency.

Margaret Alfrey has experience of teaching across the primary sector, specialising in English and mathematics. Until last year she was the Dean of the Faculty of Education at Canterbury Christ Church University College. She has particular interests in child development and developing alternative routes into higher education and teaching. Margaret has worked in Kent and the London Borough of Newham with licensed, articled and graduate teachers and, more recently, is developing collaborative provision of a Foundation Degree with LEAs and institutions of higher education.

Chris Carpenter trained at Loughborough University. He worked as a PE teacher in four maintained schools for a number of years. Chris also ran INSET as part of the TOPS programme and worked part-time as an advisory teacher in Oxfordshire. Now a senior lecturer at Canterbury Christ Church University College, Chris is course leader for the PGCE secondary Physical Education programme. Chris's main research interests are formative assessment and establishing teacher and pupil perceptions about learning in physical education.

Helen Conder trained and teaches in Kent. With a Natural Science degree in Education and several years as primary school science coordinator as well as a personal interest in environmental matters, Helen has theoretical and practical experience in science in the curriculum. She has a passionate interest in bringing 'real-life' science and classroom science together in ways that are beneficial and meaningful and which can suitably equip individuals to engage in topical debates which inevitably affect their lives.

Jenny Crisp trained in Nottingham and taught in Leicestershire Primary schools before moving to Kent. She spent some time in the Advisory Service as well as working as a SENCO and Senior Teacher. Now employed as a Senior Lecturer in Education at Canterbury Christ Church University College, Jenny teaches on Initial Teacher Training Courses as well as on the Foundation Degree in Children and Young People Learning where her chief interests are behaviour inclusion and the work of Teaching Assistants.

Gina Donaldson worked in primary schools for 11 years as class teacher, mathematics coordinator and then deputy head. She was trained as Leading Mathematics Teacher. She joined the primary mathematics team at Canterbury Christ Church University College in 1999 where she teaches undergraduate and graduate initial teacher training programmes, and a range of Continuing Professional Development courses for teachers and subject leaders. She has a particular interest in the role of the primary mathematics subject leader, and children's problem-solving strategies.

Jackie Durell trained as a mature student in Kent, specialising in English and psychology. During a varied professional career she has taught pupils from nursery age to 'A'-level, including eight years as a head teacher of a primary school. Since joining the staff at Canterbury Christ Church University College, she has developed and maintained interest and expertise in alternative routes into teaching, having worked with Licensed and Articled teachers. Her current involvement is primarily with the Foundation Degree, enabling people from non-standard backgrounds to obtain a degree and to enter teacher training.

Derek Greenstreet taught in primary schools, before becoming head teacher of two schools and then moving into teacher education. He has been a principal lecturer in primary education in the Faculty of Education at Canterbury Christ Church University College and has also had extensive experience of leading in-service work in schools. His interests are in visual education and the quality of the learning environment created in the classroom. He has published two books on the subject and contributed to a number of national reports relating to visual education.

Clare Holloway trained in Bath and taught in primary schools in Kent. At Canterbury Christ Church University College she is a senior lecturer on both the Foundation Degree and BA (Hons) programmes. Over the past two years her specific interests have been in language and cognitive development in the early years.

Lynn Revell is a specialist in Religious and Citizenship Education at Canterbury Christ Church University College. She has been a primary and secondary teacher and has written materials to use in schools for all Key Stages in these subjects. She is currently researching in the area of values and education and is a consultant for Kent Police for Citizenship Education and the law.

Christine Ritchie came to Canterbury Christ Church University College following a career in schools working with early years and primary children. Christine is a senior lecturer working on the Foundation Degree and its progression route the BA (Hons) Child and Youth Studies. Christine's interests include the development of study support strategies, particularly those offered to mature or distance learners involved in widening participation programmes, such as the Foundation Degree.

Guy Roberts-Holmes was a primary school teacher in the Inner London Education Boroughs of Southwark and Tower Hamlets for several years. He completed his doctoral studies on Gambian Teachers' Lives and Careers while doing Voluntary Services Overseas (VSO) in West Africa. His current research interests lie within the rapidly developing field of childhood sociology. Specifically these interests are inclusion in education and the sociological processes of identity formation within childhood.

Sue Soan trained as a teacher in Portsmouth, specialising in History and Mathematics. She has since taught in East Sussex, Shropshire and Kent, first, as a class teacher and subject coordinator and then for the last decade as a SENCO in mainstream schools, a MLD Unit and a specialist EBD school. At Canterbury Christ Church University College Sue is a Senior Lecturer in Enabling Learning. She is particularly interested in the areas of social, emotional and behavioural difficulties and in children's motor control development. Sue has also recently been part of a team carrying out research into 'behaviour for learning' for the TTA.

Steve Varley began training as an architect and this has sustained his interest in Art and the environment. He trained for teaching at Canterbury Christ Church University College and taught in Kent primary schools before returning to the University College as Senior Lecturer. His practical art experience led to early involvement in, and later responsibility for, initial teacher education in Art, Craft and Design. His other contributions are in language and literacy and professional studies, He is currently coordinator of the fourth year of the undergraduate programme and leader of primary employment-based routes into teaching.

Kevin Ward trained and taught in London and Canterbury before joining Canterbury Christ Church University College. He has a specialist interest in the fields of science and design and technology education and the role and use of ICT in schools. Kevin is a Senior Lecturer and is currently engaged in delivering a number of courses on the Foundation Degree in Children and Young People Learning.

Beryl Webber is an independent mathematics consultant who has written many books and is presently working with Canterbury Christ Church University College on the Foundation Degree. She also supports schools working with PGCE students and is a consultant for the QCA. Starting as a teacher in primary and secondary schools, she went on to work as an LEA adviser, introducing the NNS to schools in Medway and has been a full-time lecturer at Canterbury Christ Church University College.

Carrie Weston has spent her career in various London boroughs, where she has been a teacher, SENCO, worked in an educational psychology and assessment service and as a SEN advisor. Now at Canterbury Christ Church University College, Carrie works in the Early Childhood Studies Department where her interests are inclusive classroom practices, issues surrounding men in the early years and aspects of motherhood. She has also written and published a number of young children's books.

Introduction

Claire Alfrey

For many people this may be the first academic book they have picked up and started to read since they left school, possibly some years ago. When the notion of university is mentioned, mature students often say that it is for young people who are academically able. They are older and have not studied for a long time, or at least not at the higher education (HE) level, and are, therefore, rather hesitant about starting work at that level. It is always reassuring to realise that there are many people in a similar situation; many of them are experienced people who have worked with children for a very long time. They have a vast practical knowledge and understanding of children but now want to know more about the 'why' – the theoretical underpinning – that will give an understanding of how children learn so that the learning support they provide is further enhanced.

This book therefore aims to do the following:

- enable people working with children to gain a theoretical perspective to underpin their work;
- give people entering higher education an academic insight into several key topics;
- encourage people to reflect upon their own practice in the light of their reading and to enable them to undertake further reading;
- support non-traditional higher education students as they embark on academic study.

Overview of the book

There are three main parts. The first three chapters consider cognitive, personal and motor development. The second four examine separate curriculum areas and the final four chapters explore the more generic issues of inclusive education, behaviour management, gender and citizenship.

Throughout the chapters we have not used the term teachers but rather educators in the recognition that many people work with children during their education. Where it has been necessary to refer to an individual, 'she' has been used to refer to the educator and 'he' to refer to the child or learner. No gender bias need be construed or constrained by this. The following section introduces you to each of the chapters and outlines its content.

How Children Think and Learn

Chapter 1 provides an introduction to how children come to understand the world they live in, and the development of their thinking and learning, mainly through the theories of Bruner, Donaldson, Piaget and Vygotsky. It examines children's understanding of their social world as well as the cognitive and cultural nature of their world and their understanding of themselves as people. Contexts in which the process of social and cultural awareness takes place and a range of possible influences on children's development are discussed.

The chapter also explores, through readers' own remembered experiences, observations, reading and discussion, the ways in which theories of development and learning explain and account for processes in development. It stresses the importance of the need for educators to observe and assess children in order to understand and promote their development and learning. A range of strategies, including identification of theoretical perspectives and their practical application in assessing children's activities, is put forward for consideration together with a summary of the implications of the chapter for educators.

Key Skills: Managing Change through Study

Facing change is a big part of embarking on a course of study and in Chapter 2 you are invited to consider the way you look at change and how this might make a difference to your approach to study. This chapter looks at the six key skills, as defined by the Qualifications and Curriculum Authority, in a general way, giving you a base from which to approach this area of academic study. A method for creating an action plan, together with recording your progress in a portfolio of work, is also suggested.

Factors Influencing Motor Development

The aim of Chapter 3 is to introduce the reader to factors which affect motor development. Landmarks of motor development in the infant are examined, as are the relationships between the development of fundamental and activity-specific motor skills. The significance of motor competence in the development of 'whole child' learning is considered and also the ways that children with different levels of motor competence are perceived as learners in other curriculum areas.

The notion of multiple intelligences is used to examine the vocabulary associated with high levels of competence in the motor domain and how this might impact on curriculum planning and teaching in school. The role of physical education in developing motor development is also considered here.

Out of the Mouths and Minds of Babes: Language Acquisition and Development

Chapter 4 considers language acquisition and development from the first sounds babies make to the varied and sophisticated uses of language made by children and adults. It aims to help you to evaluate the role of non-verbal and pre-verbal communication in the development of spoken language and explores the ways in which we all enhance our conversations with a silent sub-text of gestures, body and facial movements.

Some of the key processes of language development are examined through various theories such as those put forward by Chomsky, Bruner and Vygotsky. Throughout the chapter the key themes are the crucial roles of speaking and listening in children's understanding and learning, and the role of the carer and educator in that process.

Children and Numeracy

The importance of giving young children a positive and confident approach to mathematics is vital. In Chapter 5 you will be introduced to the development of mathematical knowledge and understanding in young children. Key issues in the teaching and learning of mathematics will be discussed, and you will be asked to reflect on your own use of mathematics in everyday life, and the way in which you learn mathematics most effectively. This should lead you to reach some principles of teaching and learning mathematics

An Introduction to Science and Technology

Chapter 6 suggests ways of thinking about science and technology in a range of learning environments, the role that learning theories have in how children learn the content of the science and technology curriculum and other issues which impact on how they learn this subject knowledge. This chapter will not give you an introduction to scientific concepts and knowledge; this is available elsewhere. However, by reading the chapter you will begin to examine and question the role, content, and place that these subjects have had at the centre of the curriculum and whether this centrality is justified.

'Mind the Gap': Creativity and Learning

Chapter 7 examines aspects of creativity allied to the situations and opportunities that would foster creative development and expression, and how children might explore and exploit activities in educational settings that indicate the emergence of creativity.

Focusing on the creative experience, identifiable patterns of behaviour in children's learning are considered. Examination of the nature and quality of the learning environment identifies the value of a rich, varied and stimulating context for learning and the importance of planning for creative growth and understanding. A brief review of the National Curriculum follows, discussing how it developed and came to be focused on measurable outcomes. It is argued that creative learning should be given status through monitoring and teacher assessment in the pursuit of a more balanced curriculum, and that children's ability to personalise learning experiences and explore innovatively and imaginatively should be encouraged in order to promote independent thought and action. Theoretical perspectives and the premise of a broad, balanced and relevant curriculum serve to validate teacher professionalism and autonomy. Children's attitudes and behaviours invoked through creative activity are seen to be essential to their success, self-image and positive contribution to the future.

Educating All: Towards Inclusive Classroom Practice for Children with Special Educational Needs

The language of inclusion is now widely used by government, local education authorities and schools in policies, guidelines and legislation. But where has the concept come from, and what does it mean for those working in schools and the children themselves?

Chapter 8 looks at the historical context and development of inclusive education for children with special educational needs. It seeks to uncover how and why so many children have been peripheral to the core concerns of education in the past, and outlines how this is changing. The chapter outlines the current requirements relating to inclusion from the National Curriculum and the Standards statements that must be met in order to gain qualified teacher status.

Managing Behaviour for Learning

The study of managing behaviour for learning is important for all educators. Chapter 9 discusses the types of behaviour that cause educators concern and provides the background to the responses which they might employ in particular circumstances. Theoretical and practical aspects are considered. It is an obvious conclusion that educators need to 'know' their learners and have constructive relationships with them. The chapter concludes that the three main notions for both educators and learners to concentrate on are: relationships, responsibility and relevance. Each of these needs to be worked on if success is to be achieved.

Gender Issues in Education

Chapter 10 begins by defining the terms: sex difference, gender and gender stereotypes. It discusses the nature/nurture debate and examines recent research on brain development, the role of family expectations, toys, popular culture, clothes and friends to try to understand the ways in which young children's gender apparently becomes fixed at such an early age.

The role of schooling, as central in the process of confirming gender stereotypical behaviour, is discussed together with teachers' expectations of children, which can be deeply gendered, and the role of children themselves in policing and patrolling each other's gendered behaviour. The chapter also focuses upon the 'moral panic' generated within the media concerning the apparent failure of some boys at school and puts this contemporary moral panic into an historical and social context, arguing that gender cannot be seen in isolation from class, ethnicity and disability issues. Finally, the chapter examines the role of gender in educational careers.

Citizenship

Citizenship Education is a new subject for schools in England. Although many schools look at related themes and topics, it has never been mandatory and they have never been inspected in relation to Citizenship Education. Chapter 11 looks at some of the reasons behind the introduction of Citizenship

Education and introduces many of the changes and issues schools will have to address as a result. It argues that not only will teachers be expected to include new material and information in their lessons but that they will also be expected to adopt a new approach to values education in the classroom.

How to use the book

Structure of the chapters

Each chapter in the book follows the same pattern with an introduction, tasks to be undertaken, a summary and key points, questions to aid reflection and an annotated bibliography.

- The introduction gives an overview of the chapter and aims which outline the key areas to be covered. The aims indicate the key areas you will have encountered by the end of each chapter.
- Tasks are set throughout the chapter. These are designed to help you reflect on the key points and to relate what you have read to an education setting or your own experience and understanding.
- Summary and key points are given towards the end of each chapter which draw out the main issues discussed.
- The questions to aid reflection are designed to enable you to relate the theory examined in the chapter to you own learning, experience and practice. They are intended to extend your own thinking and understanding of the issues put forward.
- Each chapter has an annotated bibliography which contains a number of books and/or websites which are useful if you wish to read further about the topics considered. Each book mentioned has a brief explanation of its content.
- The bibliography lists the details of the books or journals quoted in the chapter.

How to get the most out of the chapters

Study habits

Every person has different study habits. Some people will study best with music, or some noise in the background, others need quiet. Depending on your personal situation, or preference, you may study best late at night or early in the morning. You may 'block' certain times during the week for time to study. You might prefer sitting on a comfortable chair or to sit at a table. Whatever your preferences or situation, you need to identify what your learning needs are in order to be able to plan to study effectively.

Reading the chapters

Do not attempt to read the whole book at one go! You don't even have to read Chapter 1 first. You might choose to look at one of the generic chapters in which you have a particular interest, such as Gender Issues or Educating All: Towards Inclusive Classroom Practice. Choose a time when you can read a whole chapter through. Read it through once without trying to make any notes, doing the tasks or trying to understand every point made. This initial reading of the whole chapter will help you get a feel for the subject and help to stop you thinking, 'Well, I don't understand that', and putting the book down before completing the chapter. There may well have been an explanation of the point you didn't understand over the page! As you become more confident, you may find that reading the introduction and summary and key points first helps you to 'tune in' to the chapter content. If this is the first time you have read an academic textbook for some time you will find that it may take some time for you to read the chapters. You will find that your reading speeds up as you get more used to the style and language of the book. Occasionally you will encounter words or phrases you don't understand. Don't be put off the chapter by this. Read around them, then make a note of them and the context in which they were used, and look them up later on. The whole aim of returning to study is to explore new ideas and to reflect on them to develop your own learning and understanding. One of our participants on the Foundation Degree summed this up, saying:

> Having to read and talk about what the children are doing and WHY has made me view my job as a teaching assistant totally differently. I have gone from seeing the school and classroom where I work in black and white and mono-sound to seeing it in full colour with surround sound! What I have read and heard on the Foundation Degree makes sense of what I am seeing and doing and I am changing what I do because of it.

You will find that the chapters have been broken down with sub-headings, this is to make the ideas and issues being discussed more manageable to follow. After you have read the chapter, you may find it helpful to note the sub-headings and write down a sentence or two which encapsulate the main points being made in that smaller section. This will help you focus on the key issues raised.

Self-belief

You may need to learn how to learn. Many of our Foundation Degree course participants have extremely high expectations of themselves. As teaching assistants they would not expect children to be able to complete a new activity or task at the first, or even second, attempt, but they do expect it of themselves! Some of you will already know how to study while some will not. Whether or not you are confident in your ability to study, this will enable you to take what you need from each chapter. However, the most important thing is that you want to continue reading, to do the tasks and complete the questions. Nearly everybody starting a degree is nervous, and perhaps those without a traditional academic background, and who have not studied for a long time, will be more anxious. This book aims to allay those anxieties and to introduce you to greater understanding of the ways in which children learn and may be supported in their learning. The words of one of our students on the Foundation Degree seem to offer a fitting end to this introduction.

> I am the first in my family to go to university. I left school at 16, like all the rest of my friends. I have worked with kids for a long time and wanted to know why they were doing what they were doing, but that would mean study and that terrified me. Watching my own kids studying at secondary school I began to think that maybe I could do it too, so I applied. When I did my first assignment I read some to my Mum, her words were 'You didn't write that, it sounds too clever!' It made me realise I could do it too!

Annotated bibliography

Cottrell, S. (1999) *The Study Skills Handbook,* London: Macmillan.
  A very accessible book which introduces the notion of learning styles and provides practical support to studying.
Ritchie, C. (forthcoming) *Successful Study: A Guide for Teaching Assistants,* London: David Fulton Publishers.
  A study guide developed for, and with, the students on the current Foundation Degree, very user-friendly.

How Children Think and Learn

Margaret A. Alfrey and Jackie A. Durell

The more condescention is made to a childes capacity, by proceeding orderly and plainly from what he knoweth already, to what doth naturally and necessarily follow thereupon, the more easily he will learn.

Hoole (1913: 6)

Introduction

This chapter will provide an introduction to how children come to understand the world they live in. It will consider cognitive, social and cultural development, giving a framework for understanding how children grow and develop. Through your own remembered experiences, observations, reading and discussion, the ways in which theories of development and learning explain and account for processes in development will be explored. By the end of the chapter you should have:

- enhanced your understanding of the development of children's thinking and learning through the theories of Vygotsky, Piaget, Bruner and Donaldson;
- understood the need to observe and assess in order to understand the development and needs of children;
- become aware of a range of strategies, including identification of appropriate theoretical perspectives and their practical application in assessing children's activities and developed the ability to use them to promote children's development and learning;
- considered the contexts in which the process of social and cultural

awareness takes place and reflected on a range of possible influences on children's development.

The educator's role

This section explores the development of children's thinking and learning mainly through the theories of Piaget, Bruner, Vygotsky and Donaldson. No theorist has all the answers in respect of explaining the development of children's understanding. Each casts some light on the problem and offers a slightly different emphasis. Some have been more influential than others and, in due course, new theorists will come along with new perspectives on human understanding.

What we are concerned with is how children come to understand the world they live in and their understanding of their social world as well as the cognitive and cultural nature of their world and with their understanding of themselves as people. It is helpful to consider this in relation to stages of development, although we must remember that we are talking about continuous development and that any attempt to relate stage to age can only be approximate. It is also important to remember that, although we may consider strands of development – physical, emotional, social and cognitive – in fact, the strands are inter-related. What we are concerned with is a developing personality.

We, as educators, need to think and reflect with academic rigour, depth and imagination on the nature of learning and above all on how children learn and how we might participate most effectively to support and enhance that process. To do this we need to recall work done with children – observing them, working with them, hearing them read, carrying out activities and other tasks – and then focus our understanding on the ways children work and interact with the theories presented, so that through sharing reflection, discussion and practice we can extend and expand the children's learning and understanding of their world.

For educators the most crucial skill is the ability to find the right 'match' between the curriculum in school and the stage the child has reached. We need two kinds of understanding for this:

1 An understanding of the subjects in the school curriculum and how teaching can be matched to the needs of the child.
2 An understanding of the way children develop and this means considering:

   (a) how far their understanding depends on their past and present experiences;
   (b) what the quality of their thinking is;

(c) how they interact through language;

(d) their personality, socialisation and the way they mix and act with others.

Obviously, we cannot think about everything but we are always thinking about something. What we want the children to do is to think more about that 'something'. We frequently hear phrases such as 'Don't think about it,' 'I can't think about it now.' Children, however, have a natural curiosity about the world around them and to make sense of their world, they need help in responding to, and processing, information they gather.

So how do theories of cognitive development help? Before we consider some theories it is useful to define what we mean by cognition and a theory. Cognition is a collective term for the processes involved in organising, handling and using knowledge and referring to all the processes of the mind that lead to knowledge, such as remembering, understanding, problem-solving, relating, imagining, creating, fantasising, and so on. A theory seeks to explain and predict and is usually based on systematic observation and experimentation. Educational theories are often based on beliefs and values about the learner, about learning itself, about the nature of knowledge and about the educator's role.

To help inform and guide us to a situation where, through planned intervention, we can provide a solid foundation of knowledge in such a way that it demands enquiry, challenge and a search for new understanding, we can draw on the work of four main theorists: (1) Piaget who refers to stages of development; (2) Vygotsky who writes of the importance of social interaction and the zone of proximal development (ZPD – what a child might achieve given the right help and support); (3) Bruner who refers to the nature of intellectual growth as equalling cognitive conflict; and (4) Donaldson who believes thinking is limited by the need for tasks and activities to make what she terms, 'human sense'. For a general introduction to these theorists, see Lee and Gupta (1998).

Drawing on these four, we might sum up learning as 'resolving cognitive conflict'. This, it is argued, is the key to achieving the aim of enabling all children to reach their potential.

Piaget

Let us start with Piaget whose theory of cognitive development is probably the best known. Although some aspects of his work are being re-examined today, his work is still of major importance to the understanding of child development. His work can be thought of as providing stepping-stones: a developmental timetable that gives approximate dates to cognitive achievements.

Piaget's stages of development

- *The sensory motor stage:* from birth to about two years (pre-conceptual). The child comes to know the world in terms of the physical actions she can perform. The stage ends with the acquisition of thought and language.
- *The pre-operational stage:* from 2 to about 7 years (intuitive). So-called because, according to Piaget, the pre-school child has yet to acquire fully logical (operational) thinking.
- *The concrete operational stage:* from about 7 to about 12 years. Typical of the primary school age child, who can think logically about 'concrete' problems in the here and now. With the acquisition of concrete operations, thought becomes 'reversible'.
- *The formal operational stage:* from about 12 years onwards. 'A form of thought acquired by adolescents ... who can think about abstract or hypothetical problems, especially in the realm of scientific reasoning, proceeding by systematic deductions from hypotheses' (Butterworth and Harris 1994, in Lee and Gupta 1998: 7).

Piaget thought children solve problems on different levels – the difference between older and younger children was not that older children have more knowledge but that they have knowledge of a different sort and a wider experience of their world. He believed children are not born with understanding ready made but that they have to construct understanding from experiences and that they have mental structures that enable them to cope with the complicated world of people and events. These structures he called schemas and the simplest of these are present at birth. For example, a baby takes in information by objects he acts on – his own fingers, toes, toys, and so on. As the baby acts on his world, he assimilates, that is, he takes in objects and events to his schemas, thereby building a store of understanding, of knowledge, for example, of faces, events, routines, food. Assimilation is, then, the process that enables children to deal with new situations and new problems by using their current stock of schemas. Children, and adults, are constantly restructuring their experiences. For example, young children may find all toys cannot easily be grasped, some won't fit in the mouth or taste tolerable, and as adults we may still be surprised at the variety of ways in which containers may be opened!

The necessary changes and modifications to our previous ways of acting on these things, Piaget described as a process of accommodation. Through accommodation existing ideas or schemas (at whatever age) become modified to fit in with the present experience and these processes of assimilation and accommodation continue throughout our life, becoming ever more complex. In a way, we construct more complex schemas by using simpler ones. This means accommodation is always the process where we undergo a mental change in order to manage problems that were at first too difficult to solve. Further assimilation and accommodation have to fit in with each other so that adaptation, or learning, can take place.

Piaget's stages

Pre-conceptual or sensory motor stage

This is not saying young children cannot form concepts. They can, and do, of shape, size, food, animals. For example, young children may work out that a dog has four legs; therefore all four-legged animals are dogs until they are told, 'No, it's a cow'. Their thinking, then, may tell them all small four-legged animals are dogs and all large four-legged animals are cows. Only later will they be classified into mammals, and so on. Equally, the usual, embarrassing or humorous example of calling all men daddy: it's not, of course that young children don't recognise their father, it's the only word they have rather than the general term male or men – a classification problem they have yet to resolve!

Intuitive or pre-operational stage

According to Piaget, children at this stage are egocentric – they are unable to see anything from a point of view other than their own. They are unable to reason in any logical way. Thinking is closely shaped by experiences without reasoning, that is, they are bound by what they see. Therefore thinking is based on perceptions and not on reasoning; it is intuitive. Parents might well turn this to their advantage: for example, when children say. 'He's got four pieces of toast, I've only got two.' By cutting the two pieces of toast in half, both children now have four pieces and all is fair! Piaget is arguing that children at this age are bound by the number of pieces of toast, always recognising that someone has more than them, not by reasoning that the same amount of toast was given to both children and merely cut into a different number of pieces. At this stage, and in the next, children are forming internal representations of their world.

Concrete operational stage

At this stage logical operations can be carried out with materials or in a particular situation with ideas and problems with which the child is familiar or can identify. Children have the ability to structure and sort out their world in the here and now but they still describe events and actions rather than explain them and they can't yet set up and test an idea – trial and error predominate.

Formal operational stage

This is the stage when abstract or hypothetical problems can be solved, when thinking is possible in terms of abstract symbols and when concepts like infinity can be entertained. At this stage, children are able to manipulate their understanding of the world flexibly and productively and separately from concrete objects or situations.

Piaget formulated these stages as a result of experiments. For example, Piaget had three model mountains, each a different shape and colour and each having something different on top: a cross, a house or snow. A child was placed near the model and a doll was positioned behind one mountain. On being asked what the doll, when moved to different positions, could see, children invariably responded with what they could see. This apparent inability to see from another's perspective changed at around the end of the intuitive, or pre-operational stage: that is, at around 7 years old. The ability to see from someone else's perspective is called de-centring. An outline of this and other experiments undertaken by Piaget can be found in Davenport (1996: 133–44).

Summary of Piaget's basic principles

1 Concept development follows an invariant pattern.
2 The child moves through several clearly definable stages.
3 Culture and environment affect age of transfer but not sequence.
4 The child must engage in activity for cognitive development to take place.
5 Conceptual growth occurs by a process of assimilation and accommodation, which leads to adaptation.

What we need to remember about Piaget's theory is that environment affects the age of transfer between stages and that all children are individuals and develop at different rates. Further, children can operate in two stages at once. For example, a child who is well able to conserve volume efficiently, because of frequently having to watch an older sibling share a can of drink between two different glasses, may well be unable to conserve number or mass, and must engage in activity for cognitive development to take place. For Piaget, development is a slow progression with children working alone as they construct their understanding.

Some of the implications of Piaget's theory

- By knowing something about the quality of children's thinking we can do as Bruner (to be discussed later in the chapter) suggests and present the curriculum in ways which are appropriate to the stage of development they have reached.

- The cultural background of children, their social and physical environment and the way in which the school curriculum is structured all have a considerable impact on cognitive development.
- Children can only understand the world through active involvement and participation in their own learning. They won't learn much by only sitting and listening. They need to be active. By active involvement we mean activity rather than passivity. The listening child is not always passive – watch the face of a child listening to a story. Equally, the doing child is not always actively involved in learning – activity can be an escape from learning or concentration.
- Concrete experiences help focus the children's minds but in the long run it is focusing the mind on the tasks that enables learning. Experiences, materials, apparatus help children see the problem in terms they can understand and with which they can identify.

Piaget's views on egocentrism and children's seeming inability to reason logically have spawned much research. However, we might question his seeming lack of consideration of, first, the context in which learning is taking place, second, 'drive' – what is it that makes children want, or need, to assimilate new ideas, and third, whether cognitive progress is the result of children's efforts to 'make sense of' and resolve cognitive conflict.

Answering these questions requires us to consider how children do, in fact, resolve cognitive contradictions – do they recognise there are contradictions in what they are told, see, or do? Are there steps towards facing, accepting and resolving contradictions and do these lead to learning? Can we speculate that, within Piaget's claim that cognitive development follows an invariant sequence of stages, it is the transfer from one stage to the next that highlights a cognitive spurt, as children resolve contradictions?

It is important for teachers to consider that there are, for both adults and children, several recognised learning styles. It is necessary to use this understanding to underpin our teaching if learning is to be maximised.

Children have preferred learning styles and we must make every attempt to offer a wide enough teaching approach to cater for a range of needs, if we, as educators, are to maximise their learning potential.

Task 1

Look at the learning styles outlined below. It is unlikely that any one will fully fit your own learning characteristics, but there may well be a reasonable 'fit'. When you have decided where you are most comfortable, compare your own preferred style in discussion with a partner.

The racer

- a tendency to rush into a task;
- a preference for getting things over with;
- optimum work is done in short sharp bursts.

If you are a racer, you will:

- start tasks quickly and with a minimum of fuss;
- easily enthuse others;
- work well when problems threaten.

You may have to develop an awareness of the need to reflect, to consider alternative courses of action, to take time to plan and to involve others more. You will also benefit from increasing your attention span.

The ponderer

- careful research of all aspects of the task;
- a tendency to re-think rather than actually getting down to work;
- given to surprise at the way 'time flies'.

If you are a ponderer, you will:

- be good at reflecting on and evaluating a task or situation;
- be creative, with good ideas;
- listen to the ideas of others.

As a ponderer you will need to be prepared to participate in discussion, taking a leading role at times. Prioritising and setting targets, as well as developing a willingness to take risks sometimes, will also be important to you.

The logical thinker

- a need to understand all aspects of the task: to make sense;
- an organised approach to problems;
- good time management and an ability to prioritise;
- a need for perfection.

If you are a logical thinker, you will be good at:

- organisation and analysis;
- problem solving;
- questioning aspects of the task.

Logical thinkers will need to develop the ability to work with others, a more creative approach to thinking and techniques to avoid stress.

The radar dish

- an interest in everything around them;
- difficulty in selecting what is relevant to the task in hand;
- a wish to see the 'big picture'.

If you are a radar dish, you will have:

- the ability to see how things connect;
- a good general knowledge;
- an enthusiastic and creative approach.

Radar dishes need to develop their skills in analytical and focused thinking, the selection of goals and priorities and the ability to edit out unwanted material.

Vygotsky

Now we turn to Vygotsky who was a Russian psychologist. He emphasised the influences of cultural and social contexts in learning and his theory, therefore, contrasts with Piaget's in that Vygotsky stressed the importance of context and social interaction and the significant relationship between language and thought. He believed that children develop cognitively through internalising processes external to them through language and social interaction – they 'talk' themselves through a problem – often directing themselves aloud before carrying out the decided action. For example, a four-year-old working with blocks and cars wants to build a roof car park. He 'discusses' with himself a range of possibilities for getting the cars up onto the roof, discarding options such as a ramp (no plank is long enough), steps (cars cannot go up steps), before going to fetch a large toy fork lift truck in which he lifts the toy car, stating that this is 'the best idea!'

Adults play a vital role in enabling children to find out what someone or something is about. They need to share children's views of the world in order to know where they are, so that they can build on the children's previous understanding. Often our ideas of children's intentions are influenced by assumptions of the right answer and our inability to share the child's view of the world. As educators, one of our roles is to enable children to make sense of the questions they are asked and of the tasks with which they are presented. We should not expect them to respond to questions or tasks which they cannot understand as they lack the necessary cognitive structures, at that stage of their development, to make sense of what we intend.

Vygotsky argued that concepts, language, attention and memory are acquired through interaction between the child and another person. For example, a four-year-old asks, 'Who puts money in there?' (the cash dispenser outside the bank), 'Do you get another someone's money?' Then looking at the notes dispensed says, 'Who counts how much is in there?' 'Can you get fifty million infinity money?', Can children get money from there?' In this sequence of questions, the adult did not re-direct attention but rather, supported the child, to enable him to come to some understanding through drawing on previous experience, not only of what the adult was about, but also what the transaction was about. The child was 'talking' himself through a problem and asking questions to help understanding.

Vygotsky believed that although children might develop some concepts on their own through everyday experiences, they would not develop abstract thought without instruction. He proposed the 'zone of proximal development' (the gap between what a child can do by independent problem solving and the level that might be achieved through problem solving – resolving cognitive conflict – with the support of an interested adult). There appears to be little doubt that children's widening circle of adults, educators, and peers help them in their search to find out what someone or something is about and helps them draw on previous experience to solve a new problem – to resolve cognitive conflict. This links with Piaget's 'stage' theory and the importance of 'knowing where the child is' in order to build on that previous understanding.

In other words, the educator/interested adult, taking a facilitating role, has to present children with situations and problems that create cognitive conflict and are right on the edge of their current understanding, which are familiar enough to give confidence so they will feel able to 'talk through' a new problem, and new enough to present a challenge demanding the resolution of cognitive conflict between previous understanding and the task presented.

What we understand from Piaget and Vygotsky suggests that, to a large extent, children's cognitive progress depends on their ability to resolve cognitive conflict. For Vygotsky, as we have seen, the stress is on the role of social interaction in cognitive development and this is heavily dependent on instruction or facilitation or teaching by adults or peers, whereas, for Piaget, the child operates to a large extent alone.

What are the key points that Vygotsky makes for us as educators?

1 To understand children we have to understand their history and the history of their culture. Adults convey to children the ways in which their culture interprets the world.
2 The importance of social interaction: complex mental processes begin as social activities and internalising those processes enables independent use. Adults and peers not only play a central role in children's learning but also significantly influence the way they see the world.
3 Learning and development are social and collaborative activities. Children construct their understanding in their own minds with adults acting as facilitators in this process. Learning needs to take place in meaningful contexts.
4 Children are able to carry out more challenging tasks when assisted by more competent people – the zone of proximal development. Challenging tasks promote maximum cognitive growth.

Task 2

Observe and then record yourself talking to a small group of children who seem highly motivated to complete a task and to a group who appear demotivated. What can you understand about their learning from their responses?

Bruner and Donaldson

The last two theories we are going to consider are those of Jerome Bruner and Margaret Donaldson.

Bruner writes of the importance of the role of the adult in 'scaffolding' to support the child in developing higher level learning skills (rather like Vygotsky's ZPD). He puts forward three ways of thinking in which we demonstrate what we understand.

- Enactive – thinking based on doing, for example, a child banging a toy to make a noise.
- Iconic – use of imagery in thinking, for example, it is easy to picture objects but somewhat limited when imagining happiness, or anger.
- Symbolic – complex symbolism, including language, freed from the constraint of actions and images.

Bruner believes we retain and use all three ways to represent our understanding throughout life, although each depends on the previous mode for its development, for example, if riding a bicycle when out of practice, we will tend to rely on aspects of enactive thought at first. However, because of our previous experience, we will be able to use imagery, for example, in deciding in advance which direction to go. Symbolic thought will enter if we describe to a friend how the 'freedom of the road' felt to us when cycling down a quiet country lane.

This means that for children to understand something they need to do it, see it, hear it and talk over with someone the conflict that shows up. For example, if five bricks are spread out to take up more space, the child's perception may be that there are now more than five. The uncertainty in the child's thinking, which is easily observable, indicates conflict in the child's mind. Children may try to count or may just look, as if thinking, 'No more bricks have been put down, but they take up a lot more room therefore …'. The conflict is, of course, eventually resolved by the realisation that, however the five bricks are arranged, there are still five bricks. Learning has taken place. (Piaget terms this as the ability to conserve number.) For Bruner it is this conflict which equals learning – and again the vital nature of the interested adult is stressed in the talking through of the problem.

Bruner states that we can present anything to a child at any age providing it is in the appropriate or right form, the right 'representation' for the child (enactive, iconic, symbolic), and that we provide the right support or scaffolding. Think of this rather like food. At certain stages, although we give a child potatoes, meat and vegetables, it is presented in an appropriate form. It's ground up or sieved for a baby, chopped up for toddlers and later presented on a plate with a knife and fork for the child to eat independently. His idea of presenting anything to a child at any age is not really simplistic. It does not mean young children can be presented with notions of nuclear physics. What he is saying is that all the basic ideas of subjects – maths, science, English – can be presented to young children enactively in an appropriate mode, making sense within their experience and later on revisited and presented in more complex forms – iconically and symbolically. For example, young children might undertake a science experiment to construct a simple circuit to make a bulb light up. At a later stage they will need to understand different types of circuits and the relation to the domestic power supply.

In summary, Bruner is saying:

1 Children learn when they have access to a supportive, interested, adult or peer.

2 Scaffolding by an adult is important for learning by providing assistance and support when children are faced with challenging tasks, withdrawing that support as competence develops.
3 Any task must be presented to children in a way appropriate to their developmental stage, and in a context which is meaningful to them.
4 Children learn by the resolution of cognitive conflict.

Margaret Donaldson (1981) argues that children, in test situations, weigh up what the experimenter says, does and may reasonably be thought to intend. Further, that problems presented to children must make 'human sense' for them to be able to solve them: that is, the problem must both connect with the child's understanding of the world around him, and be presented in language with which the child can 'connect'.

In school, children respond to questions according to what they perceive as the teacher's expectations of them. This means the child's interpretation of words is influenced by his expectations of the situation. Previous knowledge is used to make sense of what is asked. We, as educators, have to ask if children understand the words in the way we intend. For example, we use indirect acts of communication in school, e.g. 'Can you shut the door?' (meaning, please shut the door, not can you?), 'I can't hear you if your hand isn't up' (meaning, don't call out) and 'shall we ...?' (meaning, 'will you?'). We also issue guidance which may confuse children, such as 'Make a line by the door', or 'Find yourself a space' (in PE). Donaldson is saying that children may not be limited in their ability to see someone else's point of view, or in their ability to understand others' intentions, when the language is appropriate and the task or instruction makes 'human sense'.

Consider this task. The educator says to a child, 'I have one cow there and one more cow here – how many cows altogether?' The child answers, 'Two cows.' 'I have two cars, and one more car, how many cars altogether?' The child answers, 'Three cars.' This is repeated with other familiar objects until, convinced the child has understood the educator asks, 'So one and one more makes ...?' The child pauses, and then triumphantly responds, 'Five!' What we have here is evidence of logical thought on behalf of the child. He is demonstrating a quite sophisticated level of logic and not only is he offering an answer and trying to make sense of the question, but he is also maintaining the flow of conversation. Responding to a question requires recognising what is being asked for, and the child here believed he had understood the adult's intentions. In his construction of the question he knows about, and can see, cows and cars and therefore can fit this into his understanding of the world, so the answer to the unknown one and one more must be different: it must therefore have a different answer. Our ideas of his constructs may be influenced by assumptions of the right answer and our inability to share our intentions with him.

Margaret Donaldson examined Piaget's stages of development and suggested that the problems presented to children must reflect the child's view of the world. Children, therefore, need to be enabled to make sense of the questions they are asked and not be expected to respond to questions they cannot understand. Therefore, not only do we have to ask if children understand the words in the way we intend, we also have to be able to read the children's intentions.

In the light of these arguments, we need to consider what may have actually gone on in Piaget's experiments. We might say, in Vygotskyian terms, there was no social interaction, no interested adult to talk through the problems presented: the tasks were too abstract and outside the children's experience (particularly the one involving mountains with snow, a house and a cross on top). Further, if children are told to watch someone moving a stick, pouring water, re-shaping plasticine, and so on, they expect it to be relevant, or to affect, what follows. Bruner would say that the children experienced conflict between what they heard and watched the experimenter do and say with what they saw. They saw different shaped plasticine, a higher water level and different alignment of sticks. Therefore, according to their stage of development, children will be bound by what they see (as in the five bricks grouped together and then spread out). A further example is the experiment where water is poured from one glass to another. Donaldson would argue that if there was an easily understood explanation as to why the liquid was poured into another glass, for example, the original one was dirty or cracked, children are more likely to agree the amount is unchanged. As we saw with the example of adding one and two cars, if children can't make sense of the question, or see a sensible reason for an action, then there must be more to the problem than they thought and therefore a different solution is called for.

Task 3

Undertake the task (for example, the teaching of positional words such as 'behind', or 'beneath', in maths, or the teaching of adverbs such as walk 'slowly', look 'sad', jump 'quickly', in English), with two separate small groups of similar ability children. With one group keep the children passive, while you demonstrate the actions. With the other group, engage the children in active involvement. Consider the level of motivation of each group, and try to assess how well each group has 'learned' the concepts.

So far in this chapter we have concentrated on cognitive development while stressing the importance of knowing the children, understanding their stage of development and recognising the importance of their environment and social world and the place of the facilitating adult in their learning. What we are going to consider here is how the process of socialisation impacts not only on children's learning but also on their understanding of their culture and world.

Socialisation

Socialisation refers to the processes whereby the standards of society are transmitted from one generation to the next. Acquiring these standards is one of the main tasks of childhood and therefore the basic issue is how children come to conform to them and eventually adopt them as their own, see Schaffer (1996).

Task 4

Try to remember your own school days. Think about children who were often chosen for 'adult' or 'teacher-led' activities, such as sport or school concerts. Now think of those who were always popular in the playground. Were they the same children? What were these children like? Now think of the children who were more isolated, who didn't seem to have many friends, who teachers didn't seem to notice much, or, indeed, those who were 'picked on' or bullied. Among the children you currently work with, do some fall into the above categories? What do you think is the teacher's/interested adult's role in such social situations?

Socialisation is adult-initiated, starting with very concrete things like, not picking your nose, being kind to the new baby, using a spoon to eat with rather than your fingers, etc., and developing to encompass the standards and norms of a particular social setting. However, the social world of children is a complex one. Families, and relationships within them, play a vital role, however, so do wider social encounters, such as child minder, school, neighbourhood and the norms of society. Therefore to understand the social lives of children, we have to consider a complexity of interrelated issues. These must include an understanding of aspects of the cultural and social life of the children we work with and their families. There are also links between socialisation and moral and cognitive development, although these are not necessarily interdependent.

Schaffer (1996: 233) summarises some models of the socialisation process:

- *The laissez-faire* model sees children as pre-formed, while the role of the parent/carer is to leave them alone to develop. Research needs to be focused on plotting the norms of development.
- *The clay moulding* model sees the child as passive, the parent/carer needing to train and shape, and the research to concentrate on the effects of reward and punishment.
- *The conflict model* assumes that the child is basically anti-social. The parent/carer therefore needs to exert discipline, while research concentrates on parent–child conflict.
- *The mutuality model* understands that the child is a participant, with the parent/carer offering sensitivity and responsiveness. Research must deal with reciprocity in social interaction.

Clearly, for our purposes, the mutuality model is the most appropriate for the vast majority of situations. You may, however, be able to think of times when this is not necessarily the case.

Task 5

Discuss within the group occasions when the mutuality model may not be the most appropriate. Think, for example of toilet training, stopping a toddler investigating the electricity sockets, or breaking up a fight in the school playground. Do group members agree on appropriate actions in situations like these, and can you fit your suggested actions into one of the above models?

To summarise the implications of the above, we need to ask what these theories mean for us as educators.

- What we do is as important as what we say.
- Tasks should be based on the familiar, matched to children's developmental stages and presented in an appropriate and varied manner, for example, the importance of children doing, seeing and talking.
- The language we use is a means of interaction that enables us to guide the cognitive processes of the children.
- We need to remember that thinking is doing, not being told, and that it is an active, not passive process.
- At any stage it is confusing and frustrating to be faced with tasks which are far beyond the current stage of understanding – the task will be dismissed as incomprehensible.

- The most satisfying experiences, and those most productive of learning, are just at the edge of the children's understanding with enough of what is new and puzzling to make them want to understand but not so new as to make the effort to understand too demanding.
- We have to appreciate the importance of a match between experiences and tasks provided and the child's level of understanding.
- We should provide children with, at whatever stage, an interesting curriculum that will challenge them without sapping their confidence and stress understanding not technique.
- Understanding and building on the social and cultural contexts of our children are essential if we are to maximise learning.

Summary and key points

It is clear from the preceding chapter that children's development in any one area cannot be seen in isolation. Every aspect of children's lives has an impact on their growing understanding of the world and their place in it. All those with whom the child comes into contact have a role to play, and teachers, who are both the instruments of a society and the tools for developing young minds, have a vital place in this arena. Their role cannot be over-emphasised.

Having read this chapter, you will have understood the ways in which children develop and come to understand their world. You will have enhanced your skills in observation, assessment and analysis of activities, relating these to your reading and discussion of theorists. You will have recognised the importance of the educator as an enabler, with the understanding and skills necessary to see where children are in order to lead them on to new areas of understanding.

Questions to aid reflection

1 How might your understanding of cognitive development theories enhance children's learning?
2 What do you consider to be the role of observation and assessment in meeting the needs of children?
3 To what extent does the process of social and cultural awareness impact on children's development?

Annotated bibliography

David, T. (ed.) (1999) *Young Children Learning*, London: Paul Chapman. This book raises some of the issues concerning children's development and learning including the centrality of parents/carers and the social environment of that process.

Grieve, R. and Hughes, M. (eds) (1990) *Understanding Children*, Oxford: Blackwell. With a Foreword by Bruner, this book explores the development of children's thinking in relation to specific areas, for example, language, communication, computation.

Rogoff, R. (1990) *Apprenticeship in Thinking*, New York: Oxford University Press. Rogoff draws on the theories of Vygotsky, Piaget and others, seeing cognitive development as occurring through guided participation in social activity with adults and peers to support and enhance children's understanding.

Bibliography

Davenport, C. (1996) *An Introduction to Child Development*, London: Collins.

Donaldson, M. (1981) *Children's Minds*, London: Collins.

Fisher, R. (1990) *Teaching Children to Think*, Oxford: Blackwell.

Hoole, C. (1913) *A New Discovery of the Old Art of Teaching Schoole*, London: Constable.

Lee, V. and Gupta, P.D. (eds) (1998) *Children's Cognitive and Language Development*, Oxford: Blackwell.

Oats, J. (ed.) 1999) *The Foundations of Child Development*, Oxford: Blackwell.

Schaffer, H.R. (1996) *Social Development*, Oxford: Blackwell.

Van der Veer, R. and Valsiner, J. (eds) (1994) *The Vygotsky Reader*, Oxford: Blackwell.

2 Key Skills: Managing Change through Study

Christine Ritchie

Introduction

Colleges and universities expect students to develop their personal performances in academic and key skills over the course of a programme of study and many will ask students to collect evidence of this progress by maintaining a portfolio of work. To do this successfully, students will need to develop an awareness of the skills required by the course, to determine their own personal starting place and then to draw up a plan to progress actively in the areas determined as being important to future academic success. As students work through their chosen course, they should be able to chart progress in developing skills and make the most of the learning opportunities available to them.

Understanding key skills is an important step towards developing an awareness of the demands made upon teaching and support staff in schools. The changing nature of an educational workplace demands that all staff develop strategies for personal professional growth. By doing so, staff are more able to support the learning of the children in their care, and become critical and proactive leaders in their chosen field.

By the end of this chapter you should have:

- considered ways of sustaining personal change through action planning;
- identified and understood the importance of developing knowledge and understanding of key skills relevant to the workplace;
- begun to evaluate performance in relation to key skill development;
- begun to consider the collection of evidence for a portfolio showing development and progression of key skills.

Looking forward to change

If you are starting on a course of study you are looking to make a change in your life. There will be demands placed upon you in addition to the demands that your lifestyle already makes, demands made of you as a parent, child, sibling, partner or employee. Although you have chosen to study, and look forward to gaining extra qualifications, you may find that this puts extra strain on you and the relationships you have with important people in your life. Learning to adapt and to keep a balance between finding time to study and enjoying family and social life will take planning, but you will find rewards in gaining new knowledge and skills and in enhanced relationships with colleagues.

Thinking about your learning and the skills that you are developing is part of these changes, and although considering key skills may seem irrelevant at times, by being aware of your development, you enhance your chances of success in your chosen study area.

Defining skills

All of us have general skills that we use in our daily lives – preparing the breakfast, driving to work, engaging in conversations – and these help us to function effectively in our personal and professional activities.

Skills are usually considered as being those things we are able to do without conscious thought, or too much hard work. They may be simply defined as any task or activity that we can do at will and to a level of competence that is predetermined. We may learn to drive a car, but once the skill is mastered it can become a free-flowing, almost unconscious activity, so much so, that you may find on some occasions that you have reached your destination without any memory of the journey! However, you may drive well, but still want to improve and join the advanced driving class, or study higher driving skills used in racing or in severe weather conditions.

Skills differ from both knowledge and understanding. You can acquire a skill through practice without necessarily having any underlying understanding of the theory behind the skill, and you can also have knowledge and understanding without having mastery of a skill. For example, I can explain in very simple terms how the car engine works, and I do understand the need to fill the car with petrol and drive safely, however, I do not have the skill or knowledge required to fix the car when it breaks down.

Working in schools requires knowledge, understanding and skill to be an effective educator of children, but we do not always have these in equal measure. Some adults appear to have the knowledge, but no real understanding or skill. Others have skills that seem to be instinctive, but lack knowledge. Recognising skills and developing them at a personal level will enhance professional growth in all three areas.

Task 1

List the skills that you possess and use in your current workplace by considering your present work responsibilities. You will find that they are varied both in the degree of skills you have, and in their importance for your work.

Now consider aspects of knowledge and understanding required to carry out your work effectively. These may be linked to specific subject areas or to the support of pupils.

Identifying skills has become an important part of our working lives. In the past, many jobs were reliant upon manual skills, with a manager telling most of the workforce what to do. Specific skills were an important factor of employment and, as long as industry remained unchanged, a vocational skill guaranteed a job for life. Thus teachers used to be 'trained' in teaching skills, and in turn trained the children in the schools. However, the workplace has changed, with manufacturing industries making way for service industries supported by new technology. Today's workforce puts more emphasis upon cognitive skills, and there is a need to be flexible, independent and creative in the workplace (DfES 2002). The government has therefore, together with industry, looked at the skills required for the future, and the Qualifications and Curriculum Authority (QCA) identified six key skills required by workplaces as being the skills to focus upon and improve. These key skills are considered valuable in all workplaces, including schools and universities, so students are expected to develop their skills as part of their studies.

The six key skills and action plans (APs)

While there are many different skills that can be identified within the workplace, the QCA has identified six main key skill areas as:

1 Communication
2 Working with others
3 Application of Number
4 Information Technology
5 Improving your own Learning and Performance
6 Problem Solving

Higher Education Institutions are increasingly demanding that students manage their own learning in these key skill areas, commonly through a portfolio of evidence. This may be collected electronically, in a folder of work, or as a combination of these two methods and may be referred to as a Record of Development.

Each key skill area is very broad, and covers a wide range of skills, knowledge and understanding so each student has to make decisions, supported by tutors, as to which area of each skill needs developing. To do this successfully action plans should include SMART targets:

S = specific	Does your AP say *exactly* what you will develop?
M = measurable	How will you know if you are successful?
A = achievable	Challenge yourself, but can you do this?
R = realistic	Do you have the resources to complete the plan?
T = time-bound	Have you set a time limit?

To begin this process, you need to consider where your starting place is by considering your strengths and weakness in the key skill areas. You can continue this process by reading further sections in this chapter, but consider the action planning process first.

Action plans are usually constructed as tables, and there are many ways of doing this. However, all action plans should be SMART, and answer in the affirmative the basic questions listed above. Figure 2.1 is an example of a layout of an action plan you could amend or adopt to suit your needs.

Recording your goals for development in an action plan not only has an advantage for the tutor and college and completes your work for a portfolio, but it also makes the chances of you developing the skills much more likely.

Skills definitions

The six key skills listed by the QCA may also be defined as different groups, or types, of skills. Thus, 'Generic' skills are those general skills that anyone needs to function adequately in today's society. 'Transferable' skills are usually described as those required by employers, as these skills can be taken from one workplace to another, used to develop new initiatives and ensure that employees can undertake work tasks effectively. 'Specific' skills are those needed to do a particular type of work and are usually offered to new employees in training packages so that they learn the skills to work effectively and efficiently in their new role. All these skill definitions have varying degrees of overlap, for example, the key skill of communication is also a generic skill required by all workers, communicating through computer systems is a useful transferable skill, whereas using sign language to communicate may be an important specific skill if you work with the hearing impaired.

Action Plan Focus
Main target area for development is:
A summary of my present knowledge, understanding and skill in this area:
What I hope to achieve:
Resources, support and strategies required:

Time scale: specific aspect of my AP	Matched to time scale: date completed:
1.	1.
2.	2.
3.	3.
How I will measure my success:	
Progress reports:	

Figure 2.1 Action plan

Communication

As a key skill, communication is arguably the most important. In your studies you will need to listen to lectures, read books, discuss issues with other students and tutors, write essays, give presentations, use email and complete a wide range of other activities which are all dependent upon good communication. You will also be engaged in a continuous intrapersonal dialogue, so remember to continue to listen to your inner voice and direct some positive thoughts inwards!

Communication, however, is generally considered a two-way process in that a message is sent and the message needs to be received and interpreted. Feedback will inform the sender that the message has been correctly interpreted, and adaptations and amendments can be added to the original message. In conversations, this process is continuous, but in other forms of communication there may be a time lag between sending and receiving. It is important that the message is as clear as possible, but all communication is problematic in that we may interpret the message in a different way from that intended.

Communication is often considered powerful, purposeful, irreversible and unrepeatable (Evans 1990). Advertising agents know the power of communicating products on television and governments know the power of propaganda. The purposes of communication include learning to build relationships with others, to help and influence others and to play and engage in experiences for enjoyment.

What you communicate, whether intentionally or not, is also irreversible – you cannot take it back – and unrepeatable – you can never duplicate the moment in exactly the same way again (DeVito 1996: 20).

If you have been away from educational studies for some time you may find it difficult to understand the 'talk' and wonder if tutors and other students speak the same language as you do. New vocabulary and new ways of expressing ideas may take a while to tune into and to understand. Whether you are reading an academic text or listening to someone speak you have to be able to 'get into their mind' and see things the way they do to comprehend and fully join in the debate – so give yourself time to 'learn the language', and be patient with yourself.

However, there is one form of communication that is used by everyone. It is the aspect of communication known as non-verbal communication. This appears to be instinctive in that we 'read' the way others respond to us or talk to us, just by looking at their body language. Albert Mehrabian in 1967 carried out controlled experiments which clearly demonstrated that non-verbal signals were more influential than any other form of face-to-face communication. It is now generally accepted that non-verbal influences, such as facial expressions, body language and eye movements account for 55 per cent of the communication between people, with words alone totalling 7 per cent and vocal influence (intonation, accent, rhythm, stresses) the other 38 per cent (Knight 2002: 66). This gives us, as humans, the means to determine when someone is lying or unsure of their facts or doesn't like you – all through picking up body language signals.

Task 2

Consider how you communicate with different people; think of the words you might use (formal, informal) the way you would behave (friendly, serious) and how this affects the way you communicate. When you have completed the activity, discuss what you have found out in pairs or in your group.

- talking with your superior in the working environment;
- talking to your best friend on the telephone;
- talking at an interview for a new job;
- talking to an older (or younger) member of your family.

In undertaking new study we communicate in some very specific ways including through academic writing and through discussion. It may be in these areas that you need to focus your action planning. Setting targets to improve your knowledge of academic reflective writing, how to structure essays or how to be assertive in discussion will help you to get the most out of your studies.

Initial questions for developing communication skills

Use these questions to help you to determine a starting place for improving communication skills.

Discussion

1 Do you engage freely in academic discussion, remain open-minded and sensitive to the views of others?
2 Do you create opportunities for others to join in discussion?
3 Are you able to summarise points, and clearly state your views with reference to academic reading and take the discussion forward?

Listening and note taking

1 Do you enjoy lectures and feel that you learn during this time, taking an active role and selecting relevant points to record as notes?
2 Are your notes helpful to you after the session, in assignments and in revision?
3 Do you organise your lecture notes in a way to help you to write essays and complete assignments?

Academic reading and writing

1 Do you use a variety of reading strategies successfully – skimming, scanning, in-depth reading – as appropriate?

2 Do you have an expanding vocabulary to help you to understand academic language?

3 Are you familiar with the college marking grid and criteria for assignments, and do you plan your work carefully to match the criteria?

4 Do you structure your work in an academic way, with a clear introduction/rationale and conclusion?

5 Is your writing free from spelling and grammatical errors?

6 Can you set out a bibliography in the style accepted for your institution?

Working with others

In all organisations we are dependent upon one another and working successfully as part of a team is beneficial to all. This is different from working in a group, in that within a team there is continuous support and positive challenge which provide motivation and interest (Balshaw 1999). To be effective and remain stimulating, teams may be made up of different personalities but all retain a common goal. One such team could be your college group. If members of the group support, rather than compete with one another, challenge without threatening and move together towards a common goal, then each member of the team will be strengthened and become more successful. The formation of the team, however, will take time and each member will have to work towards that end.

In examining how teams are formed, Handy (1990) explores the rules that teams set for their members. These rules vary from team to team, but help to bind the members together, although the rules themselves remain unwritten. Such rules are usually related to the behaviour of the group with behaviours associated with a willingness to take on extra tasks, or join in discussion, or share resources being favoured, and those considered inappropriate, such as arriving late, not contributing to the group, demanding too much tutor time, being punished.

Task 3

Which groups or teams do you belong to? What are the unspoken rules of the group and how would you know if you had broken these rules? How would the team reward or punish team members?

Teams also appear to develop a hierarchy, in that some members always take on certain roles. This becomes accepted by the team and it can be difficult to change roles once they are established. You may notice that one person in the group becomes the spokesperson, or another takes responsibility for collecting information. There may be many members of a team, but Handy, makes the different roles within a team simple, in that he states that 'Four are enough for me' (1999: 126). These four members required by any team are the Captain, the Administrator, the Driver and the Expert. The role of the captain is, of course, to be the leader of the team, the administrator keeps the records, the driver makes sure that members fulfil their tasks, and the expert is the person members turn to when they need the answer to a question.

Task 4

Observe a group at work and see if you can spot the captain, administrator, driver and expert roles. These roles may be passed between different people, and some people will try to take on more than one role.

Set up an observation task in groups of six people. You will need newspaper, scissors and sellotape. The group task is to produce a newspaper bridge. You can set criteria if there is more than one group taking part. For example, you can have a competition for the strongest bridge, or the most elegant bridge.

One member of the group takes on the role of silent observer. In Figure 2.2, a record can be made of the behaviour of the members of the group to note how they take on the four different roles associated with teams.

Handy (1999) suggests that teams have a life of their own and that they change over time. He observes that you can watch teams *forming*, as the members get to know one another. Following forming, teams begin *storming,* where individuals begin to assert themselves and take on their active roles. This in turn is followed by *norming,* when the teams begin to settle down to a way of working together, and it is only after this stage that teams can begin *performing* and carry out the work the team was created to do. You may have noticed these stages in carrying out the observation above.

In considering the key skill of team working, you should look at the way you interact with others, both at college and in your workplace, and note how you can become a more effective member of the team. Certainly, some teams seem to be more effective than others and the reasons for this may be varied. However, Lacey and Lomas (1997) identify some of the characteristics of successful teams which you could use to identify such teams:

- A good team leader: gives clear direction, is flexible and adaptable.
- A supportive internal environment: allows for the differences between individuals, without fear of criticism or being ridiculed, and creates an 'open climate' in which to operate.
- Mutual trust: information is shared and discussed and confidentiality is maintained.
- A good system of communication: members can talk openly, and there is an agreed system for recording and circulating information.
- Clear agreed objectives: all members of the team have a commitment to the goals and objectives agreed by the team.
- Utilisation of members' resources: the ability, skill, knowledge and experience of all members are fully recognised and used.
- A supportive, external environment: the place where meetings take place is comfortable, secure and without undue distractions.

(adapted from Lacey and Lomas 1997: 114–49)

Working as a team can be viewed as an important aspect of your studies in that you will need to negotiate with your team at work, your family team and your study group to be able to manage effectively the tasks required to complete the academic course.

Initial questions for developing working with others

These questions may help you to devise action plans to develop this skill–

1 Do you behave in a way that is supportive of the team by making your needs clear, but contributing to the needs of others and by adhering to the accepted behaviours of the group?
2 Do you generally know what you want to say in the teams that you work with? Do you know which member of the team to talk to?
3 Do you have all the relevant information required to contribute to the team?
4 Are you able to gain the attention of the team, or members of the team?
5 Do you know your role within the teams where you are a member?
6 Are you able to handle conflict within the team successfully?

Application of number

Aspects of number exist in all human activities, but you may have thought of number only as a means to complete difficult abstract calculations. In considering the key skill of application of number, there is a need to be able to be competent in calculations, but it is the use of data and the application

1. Are people taking on different roles? If so describe these roles. (e.g. Captain? Administrator? Driver? Expert? Other?)	
2. How methodical/effective are the strategies used to work towards the outcome in:	
identifying a strategy?	
monitoring progress?	
evaluating outcomes?	
preparing for and presenting outcomes?	
3. What skills are being used by the team members? (e.g. negotiation, identification of expertise, assessment of effectiveness, cooperation, exchange of information, etc.)	
4. Any other comments?	

Figure 2.2 The observer's brief

of number which is present on a daily basis that are more important. Number is explicit in our daily lives as demonstrated by the need to budget satisfactorily to purchase resources, to estimate quantities for preparing food, to estimate shape and size when selecting clothing, as well as a wide range of other daily activities.

Establishing opportunities to use number skills and then evaluating the results, including interpretation of findings from your work, are part of the skills needed in this area. Within an academic framework this may involve presenting data from a questionnaire or research findings to support your writing.

Task 5

The purpose of this task is to assess different ways of presenting data. Here are the steps that you need to follow to complete this task:

1 Decide on a source of data and consider how the information is to be collected (this could be noting the shoe sizes of group members or collecting preferences for food, or any other similar data).
2 Process and analyse the data. (What information do you have? What does it indicate?)
3 Record the data, using a method of your choice (pictogram, bar graph, pie chart, line graph, frequency table, Venn or Carroll diagram).
4 Consider and collect the mathematical vocabulary that you use.
5 Consider what the data can tell you, what it does not tell you.
6 Create a set of questions that you can ask about the data.

Compare the different ways in which groups present their findings – are some methods clearer or more appropriate for the data than others?

In using the skill of application of number you will also be using other key skills, for example, information needs to be communicated and Information Technology may be used to present the findings. You might also need to follow alternative lines of enquiry and thus engage problem-solving skills. As you question and evaluate your use of application of number, the process will involve aspects of improving your own learning and performance. In this way application of number can be seen as being truly universal.

Initial questions for developing application of number

1 Are you aware of opportunities to develop number skills in your course work?
2 Do you feel confident in using/collecting data, creating a spreadsheet, creating tables and thus presenting your findings in a variety of ways?
3 Are you able to use fractions, decimals, percentages and ratios to convey information in assignments where appropriate?
4 Are you confident that your basic mathematical knowledge will support all the work that you need to do on your course? Are you taking actions to improve where necessary?

Information Technology (IT)

Information Technology, the use of computers and related software, is an important part of any higher education course. Many universities require that all assignments are word-processed, although many accept handwritten assignments for a limited period of time as students learn to use the technology. The growth of IT as an enabling technology for learning has been increasing rapidly with many new opportunities to communicate and access information becoming available to both on-site and distance learners.

As a student you may well find initially that you feel surrounded by information and demands to use information technology. Action plans should be created to identify and prioritise the skills that need to be developed, linked with the resources required and a timetable. Training may be available from your institution or on-line to assist you.

Using word-processing software to produce assignments also includes learning how to set out your work to institutional requirements, remembering to save and back-up all your work to avoid accidental loss, and how to set out references in a table, for example, as in a bibliography. You may also be required to set up and use spreadsheets or graphs within your work. The work can then be presented in a professional manner, provided that you have proof-read to check spelling, grammar, labelling of charts, diagrams and graphs accurately.

All academic work will require efficient searching and selection of relevant information, much of which can be accessed through the Internet or your institution's library resources. You will not only need to find the information, but also evaluate and compare different sources and decide if the information is relevant and reliable for your needs. There is a bewildering array of material available via the Internet, but do remember that not all of this is accurate or reliable. Try completing the activities available from 'The Internet Detective' (http://www.sosig.ac.uk/desire/internet-detective.html) to assist you in assessing Internet sources.

In addition to word-processing and research, your institution is likely to have a range of communication tools in place, such as email, web-board or a virtual learning environment that encourages students and tutors to support learning and give advice at a distance. Computer conferencing or message boards are able to facilitate discussion and can greatly enhance learning opportunities, especially for part-time students. However, regularly checking such systems becomes important and the system can only be as effective as the people using it. Students need to learn how to log on and use passwords, and also where to get help from if there is a system failure from a home or outside computer.

Improving your own learning and performance

In developing this key skill, students need to take an active part in establishing opportunities to improve their performance in all the other skill areas. In particular, by developing and maintaining action plans and ensuring that all learning targets are SMART targets. It means making a conscious, sustained effort to improve in all areas, managing time and resources effectively and evaluating and assessing your learning in a systematic and organised manner.

To do this effectively you should understand your own current capabilities, including your preferred learning style. In understanding your current capabilities, consider the four levels of learning leading to unconscious competence, see Figure 2.3.

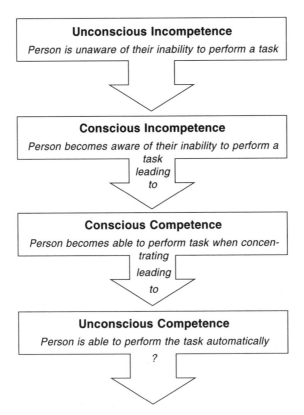

Figure 2.3 Unconscious competence
Source: Adapted from Shaw and Hawes 1998: 32–3.

As you looked at Figure 2.3 you may have been able to identify a time before you really knew what was involved in performing a task, such as driving a car, and can trace the different stages until the time came when you could drive and talk at the same time, as described earlier in this chapter.

Interestingly, becoming 'unconsciously competent' is not the end of learning, as you may be driving the car competently, but may be unaware of some aspects of driving until put into a new, challenging situation. In this respect, we are moving between conscious and unconscious competence constantly; there is always something new to learn and learning never ends.

Task 6

Look at the descriptions of learning styles below and decide which one best describes you. You may find that you say 'yes' to several questions, but look for your most dominant style: the set of questions that you feel instinctively describes you.

Visually-orientated learners

- Do you write down words, use lists, diagrams, mind-maps to help you remember things?
- Do you find it difficult to sit down and listen for long periods of time?
- Do you forget names of people and places, but remember faces and images?
- Do you like pictures, posters, videos, wall-charts to help you to learn?

Auditory-orientated learners

- Do you sound out words when spelling, enjoy listening but also want to talk?
- Do you respond well to lectures, audiotapes, and like verbal instructions?
- Do you thrive on discussion, telephone conversations, and argue with the computer?
- Have you got a good memory for names, but sometimes forget faces?

Kinaesthetically-orientated learners

- Do you 'talk' with your hands and write down words to see if they look right, and keep on talking while continuing with an activity?
- Are you impatient to 'have a go' yourself, and prefer hands-on activities to discussion or passive viewing?
- Do you easily remember the activities and events you shared with other people?
- Do you prefer reading non-fiction, avoid reading novels, and tend to ignore given directions and instructions and prefer to figure things out for yourself?

Source: adapted from Rose 1987

In understanding your preferred learning style you need to understand yourself. We receive and process information continually as we are learning through our five senses. However, individuals vary in the way they learn and retain information, and construct new knowledge. Some people engage in internal dialogue, some create a mental picture and others tend to experience the world through their feelings and a 'hands on' approach. Generally, these are referred to as visual, auditory and kinaesthetic-orientated learning styles. In reality, we probably use a mixture of all three learning styles in varying degrees according to the context for learning. However, finding out what is your preferred learning style means that you can direct your study to that style and become more effective in learning and acquiring new skills and knowledge. Many extensive questionnaires are available on the Internet to help determine individual learning styles and you could discover your own learning style by completing one on the website http://chaminade.org/inspire/learnstl.htm or at http://www.howtolearn.com/personal.html. Here is a brief overview to make a quick assessment of your own learning style.

In developing each key skill the student should take responsibility for enhancing personal performance. Do this by exploring the opportunities provided through study to strive for greater competence in a systematic and structured way. Identify future learning, personal or career goals and work towards these by selecting methods that will help you to achieve the quality of learning desired.

Problem solving

As a student you will often have problems with assignments or time management or in other areas of professional practice. One of the main factors in problem solving is identifying the problem correctly in the first place. Once a problem is recognised, it can be divided into a number of smaller problems that can be tackled singly, or help can be sought from others. If you have identified the root cause of the problem, it is wise to consider several ways of solving the problem, and not just choose what appears to be the first and perhaps the easiest option. If you write down the problem in a clearly defined way, and then get others to look at the problem with you, more solutions may be suggested. A measured choice can then be made, choosing a solution that will correct the problem in the direction to which you wish to go. However, this should not be the end of the process, as you should continue to monitor the situation and ensure that the problem has been solved, not merely hidden.

Here is an overview of the stages to problem solving:

1 Recognise and define the problem; divide into sub-problems.
2 Decide where you want to be (how will it be without this problem?).
3 Identify possible solutions; share with others, seek support, consider different methods of solving the problem.
4 Carry out the solutions; apply the methods selected.
5 Evaluate and review the effectiveness of the solutions, adapt as necessary.
                                                    (Adapted from QCA 2001: 50–1)

Methods of problem solving revolve around ways of promoting creative thinking. This can be in a written form such as brain-storming, mind-mapping or carrying out a SWOT analysis by looking at the strengths, weaknesses, opportunities and threats of any possible solutions. Usually a quadrant is drawn up when undertaking a SWOT analysis, see Figure 2.4.

Draw out a blank SWOT form, and in answering the questions, along with others that you think of as you progress, you can begin to determine whether a course of action is the right solution to your problem.

Strengths	Weaknesses
What are the advantages? Could you do this well? What are your skills in this area? What are the resources/support structures that you can use? How reliable/ permanent would this be?	What should be avoided? What might go wrong? What costs will this incur on time, resources, etc.? Who would you upset? Would the solution last?
Opportunities	**Threats**
Where are there chances waiting for you? Who could you go to for help? What positive change would this make? How would this help you in the future? Where is it going?	What obstacles do you face? Is there a real lack of resources/ willingness to help? Where will this lead you in the future? Who/what will stop you? Will this cause difficulties in other areas?

Figure 2.4 SWOT analysis form

In problem solving, the saying, 'two heads are better than one' certainly applies. As individuals we may be too close and too emotionally involved with the problem to see the solution clearly. Using communication skills to discuss problems and working as a group to find solutions may mean that several ideas, rather than one idea, are generated by the group.

Recording key skill progress

Many higher education institutions require students to maintain some form of record of key skills development to enhance progress and to provide evidence of personal achievement. Such a record must show development over time, so it is important that entries are made regularly and these are carefully dated. Within each key skill area this progression may be shown through three major stages of development, as detailed in the QCA key skills documents (2001, 2002):

1 Developing a strategy
   This is the first stage when students should collect information that establishes their current capabilities and identifies the targets to be reached. It will also be necessary to spend time researching and exploring opportunities for improvement in the key skill area. This may be through training, personal study and reading, or any combination whereby the student seeks support and resources to enhance professional development. Once the different opportunities have been assessed, decisions can be made taking account of personal preferences, needs, motivation and circumstances and an action plan can be formulated. The action plans should leave room for changes and for progress to be recorded as steps towards the target are reached.

2 Monitoring progress
   Notes on how time is managed to enable students to prioritise, organise and monitor their tasks should be recorded. Independent learning strategies which lead to improvement such as reading, discussion, information technology-based exercises, lecture notes and watching video, should be recorded and dated. In addition, students should reflect critically on their learning experience by thinking about particular experiences and noting how any particular action resulted in change. A log or diary could be used to record reflections. Students should also seek reliable feedback from others to monitor performance and help in making informed decisions for future actions.

3 Evaluating the strategy
   If a strategy is used to improve performance, then evidence should be collected as a way of presenting achievement. Key aspects of learning, how skills have been adapted and used, factors that have impacted on learning, levels of confidence and the perceived strengths and weaknesses of their work should all be linked together to demonstrate the effectiveness of strategies adopted and to illustrate new learning. Finally, this section should look forward to the future and suggest further ways in which improvements could be made.

Henry Ford, the motor car entrepreneur, once said, 'If you think you can or you think you can't – you're right', which to me, sums up the philosophy behind the issues of key skills. Improving your performance in all academic areas is about structured, effective management of time and hard work, but most of all it is about your belief in your own abilities to learn and to change.

Furthermore, in recording your progress you are increasing the likelihood of success. The written word is powerful, and when written with careful, directed purpose, can create a belief in the individual that will motive and direct learning towards concrete and long-lasting experiences.

Summary and key points

The key skills have been examined in turn, and you have learned how determining your own current capabilities and creating Action Plans with SMART targets will help you to progress in each area. Making the most of study opportunities by being aware of your learning style, strengths and weaknesses will focus learning and ensure quality of outcome from the learning experience.

This chapter also looked at ways of recording progress through developing strategies, monitoring progress and evaluating strategies through the maintenance of a record of development. This was shown to be an effective way of collecting evidence and enhancing success. Such evidence not only illustrates individual progress, but also increases the chances of long-term learning taking place because learning outcomes have been made explicit.

Questions to aid reflection

1 List the ways in which you learn best in different situations. How can you use this personal knowledge to ensure you make the most of your course of study?
2 What are the six key skills identified by the QCA as being the most important workplace skills? How do these key skills fit in with study and how will the action plan help in the process of acquiring and developing skills?
3 How can you evaluate your own performance, and chart your development in key skill areas? How would you manage a portfolio of evidence to demonstrate your progress?

Annotated bibliography

Handy, C. (1999) *Inside Organizations,* London: Penguin Books Ltd. An easy, enjoyable book to read that details aspects of the workplace culture, including how teams are created and function effectively.

Buzan, T. (revised 2000) *Use Your Head,* London: BBC Worldwide Limited. Ways of thinking, learning and problem solving using your brain in a creative but natural way!

QCA (2002) *Key Skills Specification and Guidance 1–4,* London: QCA Publications.

These documents are also available on-line:

http://www.qca.org.uk/keyskills/

Internet sources

http://www.sosig.ac.uk/desire/internet-detective.html

This website is a good starting place for discovering the advantages and disadvantages of website information.

http://www.ldpride.net/learningstyles.MI.htm

Learning style website to explore, or use a search engine to find a questionnaire or information that suits you.

Bibliography

Balshaw, M. (1999) *Help in the Classroom,* London: David Fulton.

DeVito, J.A. (1996) *Essentials of Human Communication,* 2nd edn, New York: HarperCollins Publishers.

DfES (2002) *An Assessment of Generic Skill Needs* (SD13), Nottingham: DfES Publications. (Also available on-line: http://skillsbase.dfes.gov.uk/ Downloads/SD13_Generic.pdf)

Evans, D.W. (1990) *People, Communications and Organisations* (2nd edn). London: Pitman.

Handy, C. (1999) *Inside Organizations,* London: Penguin Books Ltd.

Knight, S. (2002) *NLP at Work,* 2nd edn, London: Nicholas Brealey Publishing.

Lacey, P. and Lomas, H. (1997) *Support Services and the Curriculum: A Practical Guide to Collaboration,* London: David Fulton.

QCA (2001) *Guidance on the Wider Key Skills,* London: QCA Publications.

QCA (2002) *Key Skills Specification and Guidance 1-4,* London: QCA Publications.

Rose, C. (1987) *Accelerated Learning,* revised edn. New York: Bantam Doubleday Dell Publishing.

Shaw, S. and Hawes, T. (1998) *Effective Teaching and Learning in the Primary Classroom: A Practical Guide to Brain Compatible Learning,* Leicester: The SERVICES Ltd.

3 Factors Influencing Motor Development

Chris Carpenter

Motor development is continuous change in motor behaviour throughout the life cycle, brought about by interaction among the requirements of the task, the biology of the individual and the conditions of the environment.

Gallahue and Ozmun (1998: 3)

Introduction

The aim of this chapter is to provide the reader with an introduction to issues related to motor development. It will examine the factors which affect motor development and also look to make a distinction between the development of rudimentary motor patterns, fundamental motor development and the development of specific motor skills. A major theme of the chapter is that motor development occurs within a particular context and that it is best understood through use of a 'wide angle' perspective. The reader should bear in mind that this chapter is aimed at students who are new to this area of study and that each of the sections is worthy of detailed examination in its own right.

By the end of this chapter you should have:

- an understanding of the nature of motor development;
- considered motor competence as a form of intelligence;
- an understanding of the relationship between development of rudimentary, fundamental and specialised movement skills;
- developed an understanding of the stages of learning of specific motor skills;

- an understanding of the role of physical education in enhancing motor development.

Key terms in this chapter

Motor: factors that influence/are related to human movement.
Motor development: the continuous change in motor behaviour throughout the life cycle.
Heuristic: learning through trial and error.
Reflexive: a movement that occurs 'automatically' and is under the control of the lower centres of the central nervous system. There is no higher brain involvement and, therefore, no 'conscious' control.

The nature of motor development

In order to develop an understanding of young children and adolescence it is best to look at matters from a variety of different perspectives such as physical factors, environmental factors and social factors. Similarly, a study of motor development also requires a multidisciplinary approach. Motor development is a valid area of study in its own right although it cuts across fields of study such as shown in Table 3.1.

Table 3.1 Multidisciplinary approach to motor development

Field of study	Definition
Exercise physiology	The study of factors affecting human physical performance.
Biomechanics	The physics of human movement.
Motor learning	The ways in which motor learning takes place.
Motor control	The ways in which the body initiates and refines the production of human motor behaviour.
Developmental psychology	Also called 'Life span-psychology', the branch of psychology concerned with the changes in cognitive, motivational, psycho-physiological, and social functioning that occur throughout the human life span.
Social psychology	The scientific study of the behaviour of individuals in their social and cultural setting.

Gallahue and Ozmun (1998: 5) identify three main areas, which will affect motor development:

- individual
- environment
- task.

While these will be discussed separately, many researchers into motor development are taking the view that the demands of particular activities will interact with the environmental and individual factors, hence the overlapping circles in Figure 3.1. This can be illustrated by considering the emergence of the East African countries in producing high quality middle and long distance runners. The socio-economic factors in many parts of East Africa are such that motorised transport is often not available. The high altitudes could mean that the population have a higher than normal number of red blood cells, which aid the oxygen-carrying capacity so essential to endurance running. The same socio-economic factors which mean that the lifestyle relies on the people being physically active also means that success in running might be a way to make a mark or even as seen as a 'way out'. Once role models are established, then the likelihood of more runners being developed from the same areas is greatly enhanced. In this way the task, individual characteristics and the environment might interact to cause particular aspects of motor development to be enhanced.

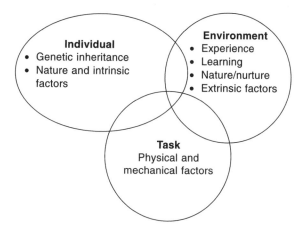

Figure 3.1 Factors affecting motor development
Source: Based on Gallahue and Ozmun (1998: 5).

In view of the importance of motor competence to survive, it seems strange that the focus of research in the past has centred mainly on the affective domain and cognitive processes. Many of the earliest indications of children's learning are in the motor domain. Lifting the head, turning to follow sounds and light, and sitting up are all significant signs of development which lie principally in the area of motor development.

Motor development should not be viewed as a process that is incremental, but rather as a continuous process throughout life and can be seen at its clearest as progression in the development of infants, and at the other end of the life span as a regression experienced by those of more advanced years.

It is also important to note that while motor development is related to age it is not dependent on age. It should also be borne in mind that progress will not be uniform on all fronts. This can be illustrated by the assertion that 'adolescent girls cannot throw'. It may be that an adolescent child might be seen to throw 'like' an infant but this could be due to the fact that they have not developed a movement skill such as the throw. They may well have the capacity to learn to throw, but have not done so for a variety of reasons. In the same way an adult may have a reading age of a ten year old. It may be that they have a particular difficulty related to learning to read or that they have not had the chance to learn as children or even studiously avoided any situations where they might be required to read!

The notion is further complicated by the fact that different physical domains may elicit very different responses from different individuals and therefore the level of perceived motor development may be skewed. Most PE teachers have met the girl who performs superbly in gymnastics and then appears a novice in invasion games. By the same token, the boy who excels in invasion games but finds little appeal in dance may present as a novice. The reasons for the differences in performance may well be a direct result of prior involvement in the activities and also the values that the children place on the activities which they have learned from the people around them. This emphasises the need to view motor development from different perspectives and not merely as a biological process which acts independently from other factors. Gallahue and Ozmun (1998) suggest there are three main elements: individual, environment and task.

Individual

A person's genetic inheritance has the potential to affect motor development in terms of the length of levers, the types of muscle fibre and also the neural pathways so essential to send messages from the brain to activate the muscle fibres.

It is axiomatic that to some extent we are 'stuck' with the physical characteristics that we have inherited from our parents. This is not to underestimate the importance of motivation, hard work and training. There has been research that suggests that black athletes have higher levels of fast twitch muscle fibres which is said to go some way to explaining the dominance of black athletes in the higher echelons of world sprinting. This is a dangerous supposition as it could be countered by the argument that if middle-class occupations, such as medicine and the law, are dominated by white people, then the avenues for career advancement through sport may seem more accessible.

The appeal of physical activity to a person's affective domain is also a significant factor. If a person's nature is such that activities in a motor domain have little appeal, there is less reinforcement to do them and therefore the levels of motor competence are likely to be less. The sheer joy of swimming, hitting a seven iron to within inches of the cup or running by the sea on a sunny spring morning may have more appeal to some than others. Those people who find them enjoyable are much more likely to seek out opportunities to repeat the experience.

This highlights the problems that are inherent in teaching health-related fitness as a discrete subject in schools. It does not reflect the diversity of human interest in movement. The importance of context in learning is well established and it seems likely that the same will apply in exercise. To highlight the exercise benefit in all areas of the physical education curriculum, rather than a focus on the traditional 'circuit training' type of activity often associated with fitness, might have more significance in impacting on children's attitudes towards active lifestyles. This in turn might encourage children to become active adults, rather than adults who are still inactive but better informed about the benefits of regular exercise.

Environment

The significance of 'nature versus nurture' in learning is a debate that has raged for many years and will no doubt continue to do so. In the introduction to this section some attempt was made to explain the prevalence of runners from East Africa and the possible 'nurture' aspects. The truth that a positivist might seek, in the case of motor development, may well lie somewhere along the 'nature–nurture' continuum. The power of the environment is widely acknowledged. Claxton (1984: 143), talking about intelligence, suggests that we view different-sized cookers being capable of producing meals of differing complexity. We are the cook not the stove. So the cooker can only be used to the limit if the cook is familiar with it and with the ingredients. Also having an interest in cooking and being prepared to experiment and make mistakes are important. Applying this to motor development, it seems logical to view our attitude as the cook and our body as the cooker. We will only develop our motor capabilities if we are familiar with our body and are prepared to become familiar with its workings and be prepared to work on it regularly.

Social groupings where physical activity is a valued part of the culture will also play a part. To be inducted into the group participation in the activity is essential, and sustained participation then becomes part of what it is to belong to that group.

The notion of exposure and attitudes is also an important element. It might be argued that Mozart was not a child genius but a child with a considerable facility for music who, due to family circumstances, had been exposed to as much music by the time he was seven as many people have been in several lifetimes. Capablanca, who was the world chess champion from 1921 to 1927, was the champion of Cuba at 12 and had spent years watching his family play chess and then played regularly himself from a very young age. There are also numerous examples of children following in the footsteps of their parents in sporting and other fields due, no doubt, to the same factors.

Attitudes to learning and activities can also be very important. Katene *et al.* (2000) found that primary teachers who were physically active themselves taught more effective PE lessons. It is not hard to see that a teacher who is committed to physical activity is more likely to ensure that the PE lesson happens and is also likely to put more work into the planning and delivery.

Bennett and Dunne (1994: 50) say that 'what children learn in the classroom will depend to a large extent on what they already know'. A child who is exposed to an environment where the role models are active and participation in physical activity is encouraged and enjoyed is likely to have significantly developed motor development *and* be in a position to access the physical education curriculum and the motor development opportunities it affords. A child who has not experienced the same encouragement prior to starting at school, and is perhaps in a family where the adults lead a more sedentary lifestyle, is less likely to be so enthused by the prospect of learning in a physical domain.

Task

The nature of the physical task has two main implications. The first being the appeal the task has to the participant. This might be affected by social and environmental factors, as outlined in the previous section on the individual. The second is the mechanical demands of the task and the physique of the performer. It may well be that this second point is only really a serious issue at elite levels of performance. Sheldon developed a system of body classification which he termed 'somatyping'. In this classification he identified three types of body: mesomorphs (tending to be muscular), ectomorphs (tending to have low levels of body fat) and endomorphs (tending to plumpness). At higher levels of performance different body types tended to allow for effective performance in particular activities. Tall people with low body mass excelling in the high jump, and shorter more muscular people excelling at the shot putt. At other levels of participation it seems perfectly acceptable for shorter people to engage in basketball and taller people to ride horses. However, it may be that a person with a tendency to a particular body type might see a particular activity as more suitable due to the role models at elite levels.

Task 1

- What physical activities do you participate in regularly?
- What is it about the activities that you find appealing?
- How did you start? Why did you start?

Can you use Gallahue and Ozmun's model to explain how it is you have come to enjoy/be proficient at the activities you have?

Motor competence as a form of intelligence

In a consideration of aspects that affect motor development, it is appropriate to consider motor competence as a form of intelligence. Howard Gardner's (1994) work on multiple intelligences is well established in the literature. Gardner identifies eight areas of intelligence, see Table 3.2.

Gardner suggests that this list is far from exhaustive and that there may be many more intelligences. It is worthwhile considering the cachet and the vocabulary that are routinely used when describing high levels of competence in the different intelligences. How often are adjectives such as *clever* used when praising good work in Maths, whereas in PE terms such as *talented* or *able* are used? What would be the result, if any, of a pupil who can perform an open somersault on the trampoline being described as clever? Would this in some way value the child's achievement in performing the somersault even more? In the long term, might this give increased value to achievement in the physical domain? Even in an age when vocational education could be an increasing feature of the Key Stage 4 provision, there is still a resonance of some subjects having their status being increased through being conferred with an 'academic' status. This is also problematic as a definition of academic in this sense is 'pertaining to an academy'. As subjects such as physical education are on the curriculum, should they be defined as academic anyway? Achievements in the physical might automatically be held in the same esteem, and might excellence be described using similar vocabulary?

If the notion of multiple intelligences has merit, should each one have parity of esteem? If this is felt to be an argument worth supporting, then this could have implications for the school curriculum. If the position is that

Table 3.2 Summary of Gardner's intelligences

Intelligence	Definition	Examples of associated career
bodily-kinaesthetic	Allows individuals to use their bodies to perform high-level motor skills.	Athletes, dancers and actors
intrapersonal	Helps individuals distinguish among their own feelings to build accurate mental models of themselves and to draw on these models to make decisions about their lives.	Therapists, counsellors, religious leaders
interpersonal	Enables individuals to recognise and make distinctions about other peoples feelings.	Teachers, politicians and salespeople
linguistic	Allows individuals to communicate and make sense of the world through language.	Journalists, novelists and lawyers
logical-mathematical	Enables individuals to use and appreciate abstract relations.	Scientists, accountants and philosophers
musical	Allows people to create, communicate and understand meanings composed of sound.	Composers, conductors, singers
naturalist	Allows people to distinguish among classify, use features of the environment.	Farmers, gardeners and geologists
spatial	Makes it possible for people to perceive visual or spatial information, to transform this information, and to recreate visual images from memory.	Architects, sculptors and mechanics

what should be valued is not 'how' intelligent, but in 'what ways' children are intelligent, then to what extent should this be reflected in the curriculum? An analysis of the school curriculum in terms of the time spent working in each intelligence is revealing. Table 3.3 shows the allocation of lessons for a Key Stage 3 pupil for the academic year 2002-2003. If Gardner's intelligences are assigned to each curriculum area (Table 3.3), a graph can be constructed which shows the amount of time that the child spent working to develop each intelligence (Figure 3.2).

The reader should be aware that such a method of assigning intelligences

Table 3.3 The number of lessons in each subject in a week for a Key Stage 3 pupil

Subject	Lessons	Primary intelligence
Art	2	Spatial
D&T	6	Spatial
Drama	1	Bodily-kinaesthetic
English	5	Linguistic
French	4	Linguistic
Geography	2	Naturalistic
History	2	Interpersonal
Maths	5	Logical-mathematical
Music	1	Musical
PE	4	Bodily-kinaesthetic
PSHE	1	Intrapersonal
RE	1	Interpersonal
Science	6	Logical-mathematical
Total lessons in a week	40	

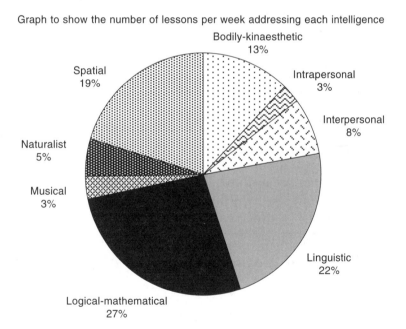

Graph to show the number of lessons per week addressing each intelligence

Figure 3.2 Graph to show the comparison between the intelligences developed for Key Stage 3

to a subject, while a useful way of thinking about the issues, is crude. In multidisciplinary subjects such as Geography, it might be argued that while physical geography is primarily naturalistic, human geography tends to the interpersonal. Similarly in Science, physics might be viewed as logical mathematical while biology might be viewed as more naturalistic. If it is accepted that the example programme is representative, then in terms of intelligences the curriculum places an emphasis on the logical-mathematical and linguistic intelligences which in this case account for almost half of the timetable time. Bodily-kinaesthetic, which is the focus of this work, is catered for in PE and Drama which account for 13 per cent of curriculum time. The issue here is not only the relative times that children will have the chance to have the various intelligences fostered by the curriculum, but also the messages this gives about the relative importance of subjects and, by implication, the associated intelligences, as recognised by government and curriculum planners.

It should be noted here that intelligences and learning preferences are not considered synonymous. It is possible for kinaesthetic methods to be employed in subjects other than PE through, for example, investigations in Science, three-dimensional work in Mathematics and role-play in English. Krechevsky and Seidel (1998: 2) draw a clear distinction between learning styles and intelligences. They make the point that intelligences have distinct developmental paths which are closely linked with achievements or valued roles in society. Children who wish to become skilled artists or mathematicians need to be nurtured in particular intelligences. One could be a tactile learner, but still become an accountant.

Task 2

- Work out the time given to each subject at your school. What does this tell you about the value of motor development?
- Talk to teachers and pupils and ask them to describe people who are good in different subjects. What adjectives do they use?
- Watch a lesson (other than PE). What types of intelligence are demanded of the children?

The significance of motor competence in perceptions of personal competence

Notions of 'a healthy body and a healthy mind' that have been handed down from the Greeks to the muscular Christianity of the late nineteenth century are well established in the literature. Self-esteem or self-concept cannot be understood unless many dimensions are taken into consideration. There are also issues of transfer. Does the fact that a person is confident in the physical domain necessarily transfer to other areas of life? If there were a transfer, under what circumstances would this occur?

Granlees *et al.* (1989) carried out a study into the importance of physical competence in perceptions of competence with primary school children and their teachers. They found that both teachers and pupils use perceived physical competence as a dimension to differentiate between boys and girls in other domains of competence. The girls tended to associate physical competence with both cognitive competence and general self-worth to a greater extent than the boys.

Marsh and Jackson (1986) investigated many aspects of self-concept in young female athletes and non-athletes. They found that across all the areas of self-concept the athletes had higher self-concept than the non-athletes with self-concept in mathematics, opposite sex relationships and emotional stability being significantly higher. These are areas where girls often have lower self-concept than boys. Marsh and Jackson suggest that for girls, involvement in athletics resulted in them being perceived more favourably in other areas.

Comparisons of teachers' ratings are also worth examining. Within co-educational classrooms it has been noted that boys and girls can come to think of girls as having different abilities and inferior status to boys and the role of teacher expectations has been highlighted in maintaining these gender differences (Evans *et al.* 1987).

If the findings reported here are accepted, then it seems possible that the messages that boys and girls are given about demonstrating and developing motor competence may be very different, even if they are transmitted in subtle ways. Even if these messages are at an almost subliminal level, then clearly they could impact on motor development. Rich (2003) in a small study involving newly qualified female PE teachers found that even though the women all claimed that the development of girls through PE was their key aim, that when teaching they reproduced some very subtle yet deeply embedded gendered inequalities.

Moving to learn – learning to move

The significance of early developmental 'landmarks', which in many cases lie predominantly in the motor domain, has been introduced in an earlier section. The importance of motor development and the access it gives children to other aspects of their development should also be emphasised here. This can be exemplified by examining established theory on child development. Jean Piaget, the Swiss psychologist who studied children's development, identified a number of developmental mileposts or phases which children pass through (these are outlined in detail in Chapter 1). Piaget suggests that higher cognitive structures are formulated through self-discovery and play which relies to a large extent on aspects of the motor domain to allow this assimilation to occur. Children therefore have to move to learn in order to be able to learn to move. This integrated view of development is similar to the case of children who are profoundly deaf and therefore have difficulty accessing language. This in turn has an impact on the development of their speech. Moving and learning, talking and listening, are inextricably linked in terms of their development. Difficulty with one will have an effect on the development of the other.

In this section it is worth taking time to think about the mixed messages that adults sometimes give children about the changing values they can ascribe to movement. In the beginning children are encouraged to speak and move and then later often in school, and at home, they are routinely required to sit still and be silent. This is not helped by a view that in some way writing in school is synonymous with learning: that sitting at a desk quietly is automatically good. Perhaps this goes more deeply and has a resonance to a view attributed to the Victorian age, 'Children should be seen and not heard.'

> The first idea that the child must acquire in order to be activity disciplined is that of the difference between good and evil; and the task of the educator lies in seeing that the child does not confound good with immobility and evil with activity.
> (Maria Montessori 1870–1952, in Sullivan 1996: 33)

It is a good time to think about learning in its widest context. While there is a tendency to think of school as the main venue for learning, it may well be that the main learning occurs elsewhere, or even that the type of learning in school is particular to school. Doherty and Bailey (2003: 3) cite Bjorkvold who outlines what could be described as a schism between the learning culture of the child and that of most schools, see Table 3.4.

Table 3.4 Comparison of child and school cultures of learning

Child Culture	School culture
Play	Study
Being in	Reading about
Testing one's own limits	Physical distance
The unexpected	Respecting boundaries set by others
Sensory	The expected
Physical movement	Intellectual
I move I learn!	Physical activity
	Sit still!

Source: After Bjorkvold in Doherty and Bailey 2003: 3

Perhaps the atomised nature of the school curriculum does not help teachers to think of incorporating elements that might enhance motor development into more lessons. The sort of thematic approaches which might have encouraged the use of different intelligences in an integrated way, as once utilised in primary schools, have fallen out of favour in recent times. As long as physical education is seen as a discrete subject, then this may be hard to challenge in a meaningful way. The use of Gardner's intelligences to review the nature of the learning activities that children are involved in might be instructive. Intelligences such as interpersonal and bodily-kinaesthetic have the potential to be nurtured in all curriculum areas if the teacher is aware and prepared to think carefully about the types of intelligence that their teaching encourages in order to access the learning required. Teaching strategies such as role play, problem solving and group discussion provide children with different ways to learn and perhaps allow children to work in preferred domains for some of the time, thus, feeling more comfortable.

In terms of social development, and learning to be part of a social group, aspects of emotional intelligence and reading physical signs are very important. Much is made at the higher levels of sport of interpreting a team's psychological state by reading their body language. In the same way, children can learn to interpret body language. Goleman (1996: 98), talking about emotional intelligence, talks about the idea of motor mimicry. He cites the example of children who can show sympathy even before they really know what it is and will mimic the response of a child who is hurt. An example would be a child who observes another child falling and being hurt. The child who observed this will cry and go to their parents for a cuddle themselves even though they are not hurt.

Rudimentary and fundamental movement abilities

Gallahue and Ozmun (1998) make a distinction between rudimentary and fundamental movement abilities. Gaining control over the muscles, learning to cope with gravity and moving in a controlled manner through space are the challenges faced by the infant. The development of motor control normally follows a clear pattern. The child will gain control of his head and gradually extend this control through the body towards the feet. At the same time he starts to develop control over the middle of the body and then extends this control outwards.

During the first months of life, the movements are ill defined and poorly controlled. Movements are reflexive in nature, which means the lower centres of the central nervous system initiate them and there is no higher brain involvement or 'conscious' control. As time passes, these reflexes are inhibited and the movements increasingly come under the control of higher brain centres. This reflex inhibition begins at birth as the infant is bombarded with all manner of sensory stimulation. The infant has to make sense of this stimulation and gradually begins to bring his responses under control. The period from 12 to between 18–24 months is a time for practice and mastery of rudimentary tasks. These rudimentary movements include abilities which may be divided as follows:

Locomotion: able to move
Stability: able to withstand gravity
Manipulation: able to make precise contact with objects around him.

Gallahue and Ozmun identify a number of rudimentary movement abilities which are summarised in Table 3.5.

Table 3.5 Summary of rudimentary movement abilities

Task	Rudimentary movement
Stability	Control of head and neck
	Control of trunk
	Sitting
	Standing
Locomotor	Scooting
	Crawling
	Creeping
	Walking on all fours
	Walking upright
Manipulative	Reaching
	Grasping
	Releasing

In the course of normal development, the infant will gradually be able to establish control over large movements and refine them into more specific movements. For example, the random waving of arms at the sight of the bottle evolves into the child grabbing at the bottle and holding it while drinking.

By around 24 months most children are well on the way to mastering their environment and have learned most of the fundamental movements. These fundamental movements then form the basis of more specific motor skills. There are many fundamental movement abilities, but they include the following:

- throwing
- rolling
- catching
- kicking
- trapping
- striking
- dribbling
- walking
- running
- jumping from a height
- vertical jumping.

It is important to note that while the sequence of infant motor development is predictable, the rate is almost always variable. The reasons for this have been outlined earlier. Environment, individual characteristics and the nature of particular tasks will all play a role in determining the rate of progress. Examples of the developmental sequences for rolling and vertical jumping are illustrated in Figure 3.3 and Figure 3.4.

It should be stressed that fundamental movements involve the basic elements of particular movement only. They do not include individual style and there is no suggestion that they be combined into more complex movement skills such as juggling with three balls or performing a lay up in basketball. Both the lay up and the juggling are skills which are composed of a number of smaller skills or sub-routines which must be combined with precise timing in order for the skill to operate effectively.

It is important to stress again that these developments are age-related but not age-dependent. The characteristics of the basic stage may well be evident in some secondary school children who have not been encouraged, had the chance, or been supported to engage in activities such as, say, throwing. The mature stage of throwing could then be employed in a number of different contexts such the overhead action of the tennis serve, throwing a javelin and the smash in volleyball. These are all examples of the mature stage being employed in a particular context which might be subject to many hours of practice and be capable of being performed with high levels of accuracy and reliability.

Task 3
- Watch children participating in physical activities. Can you see developmental stages in any of the fundamental movement abilities?
- Talk to children to get an idea of their background in physical activity. How does this affect their work in school PE lessons?

Initial

Mature

In the initial stage there is no sign of taking the ball back to prepare. The roll is made without transferring the weight towards the target.
In the more mature stage the body is turned sideways on to allow the arm to go back easily and the hips and shoulders to turn to allow the arm to come through vertically so giving the best chance of a straight throw.

In the initial stage the follow through goes up into the air and there is no sign of the body weight having been transferred in the direction of the throw.
In the more mature stage the arm is 'on line' towards and the body weight has transferred to the front leg.

Figure 3.3   Developmental stages of rolling a ball

The relationship of fundamental movement abilities to learning more complex activity specific skills

Once fundamental movement abilities are secure, activity specific skills may be learned. Fitts and Posner identified three stages in skill development:

- cognitive stage
- associative stage
- autonomous stage.

Figure 3.4   Developmental stages in a vertical jump

Cognitive stage

The learner is trying to get to grips with the nature of the activity to be learned. Demonstration is important, as are verbal explanations to highlight important cues. The learner is trying to understand what to do and how to do it and it often helps to verbalise. Full concentration is needed and performance is full of errors and the movements are inconsistent and lack fluency.

Associative stage

The learner now understands the aim of the activity. Movement patterns are well integrated and automatic. Simple aspects are well learned and there is the possibility of refining them into more complex ones. The learner now 'feels' the movements with the end result. Feedback should be specific and should focus both on knowledge of performance and knowledge of results to allow the development of kinaesthetic feedback.

Autonomous stage

The movement patterns are now well integrated and automatic. The performer has sufficient 'spare attention' to concentrate on the external environment. There is less need for external feedback as the learners can correct themselves. What feedback there is from external sources can be detailed and specific. An example of a skill performed at the autonomous level would be driving a car. The driver is able to perform all the actions needed to move the car and is able to concentrate on the external environment in order to make the journey safely.

These stages are not discrete. Rather, they describe the characteristics of the stages that the learner will pass through in learning specific movement skills, see Figure 3.5.

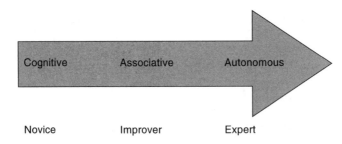

Figure 3.5 Diagram to show the progression through the stages of Fitts' and Posner's model

In Table 3.6 an example of a person learning to juggle is described in terms of the stages of skill learning outlined by Fitts and Posner.

Table 3.6 Fitts and Posner exemplified through learning to juggle

Fitts' and Posner's stage	Characteristics of performance at each stage
Cognitive stage	In this stage the learner has to think very carefully about how to start the action, e.g. two balls in one hand and the third in another. Much thought is needed before one ball is thrown. The cycle is usually not completed. The learner still has difficulty visualising the 'whole' skill.
Associative stage	The cycle is occasionally achieved with poor control. The learner understands the sequence that the balls must be thrown. Frequent errors both of timing and the basic sub-routines of catching and throwing break down easily.
Autonomous stage	The balls are juggled consistently and the learner has 'spare attention' to focus on other tasks such as speaking and listening. The sequence only breaks down when boredom, fatigue or a lack of attention occur.

Task 4

- Think about your own motor skills. Can you identify a motor skill for each of Fitts' and Posner's stages?
- Watch a lesson. Can you identify children who are at each stage of the Fitts and Posner model?
- In what ways might a knowledge of Fitts and Posner guide the teacher's interaction with the children?

The role of physical education in enhancing motor development

There seems little doubt that physical education is the principal subject involved with motor development in the school curriculum. The challenge for the physical educator is to have a sense that the purpose of the lesson is more than inducting children into the playing of culturally valued games such as netball and rugby. This is an impoverished view of what the physical education lesson can offer. This convergent approach can be less than helpful in terms of allowing all children to have access to the curriculum and also in terms of the motor development opportunities. John Parsons, a physical education HMI, refers to the aims of PE as to 'produce people who can become performers of, rather than to produce performers of'.

There is also a sense that there should be a 'meta' level of understanding about movement in the PE curriculum. A learning *about* movement as well as learning *to* move focus.

Stewart suggests that in terms of developing children with delayed motor development the programme should contain the following:

- repetition
- frequency
- variety
- emotional impact on the learner.

The appeal to the emotional, or what Laker (2000: 22) refers to as the 'affective domain', is an essential ingredient in a physical education programme, especially if the 'lifelong active habits' that are claimed by the mission statements in many PE departments have any chance of coming to fruition. It seems logical to apply the same criteria to all children in terms of motor development in schools, both primary and secondary. Insufficient attempts will affect not only the motor development, but also children's self-esteem about how they are progressing. Failing to secure learning is an issue in all subjects.

The British Association of Advisers and Lecturers in Physical Education (BAALPE) defines physical education as consisting of physical skills, personal and social skills and learning skills. Motor development in this context would be a product of developing personal physical skills and learning how to learn in the physical domain in a formal social context.

The core strands in the National Curriculum for PE direct teachers to develop children's abilities to do the following:

- acquire skill;
- select and apply;
- evaluate and improve;
- have knowledge of health and fitness.

This notion of acquiring skill and understanding about movement through having the chance to make decisions and learn from them through evaluation is a powerful model for learning. It encourages teachers to allow children to learn in a heuristic manner. This active involvement and exploration when combined with effective feedback from the teacher allow the children to 'reconstruct' their understanding about movement and develop new and more challenging patterns in the context that they will be used. The 'Games for Understanding' approach where the child is taught through the use of appropriate game forms is a good example of this.

Summary and key points

Motor development is a continuous change in motor behaviour which occurs throughout life. It is affected by the environment, the nature of the motor challenges that the learner is presented with and the personal characteristics of the learner. Therefore, it is important to consider a range of issues when examining this area of study.

If Gardner's work on multiple intelligences has any credence, then perhaps high levels of competence in the motor domain should be viewed as a form of intelligence and given equality of esteem with the traditional academic intelligences, both in terms of the regard that society has for them and the school curriculum.

Questions to aid reflection

1 In the light of this chapter, consider aspects of your own motor development. What factors have combined to cause you be at the level of motor competence that you are?
2 What do you feel is the place of motor development in the overall learning of the 'whole child'? How might this change with age?
3 What do you feel are the values ascribed to motor competence compared to other domains? Why do you feel this happens?

Annotated bibliography

Doherty, J. and Bailey, R. (2003) *Supporting Physical Development and Physical Education in the Early Years,* Buckingham: Open University Press. This book is a useful guide to the place of motor development in the learning of the 'whole child' and states the case for the place of physical education in the early years.

Gallahue, D. and Ozmun, J. (1998) *Understanding Motor Development,* New York: McGraw-Hill.

This is an extensive textbook which covers the ground of all aspects of motor development in detail, and is essential reading for students who wish to develop this as an area of study.

Gardner, H. (1994) 'The theory of multiple intelligences', in Moon, B. and Shelton-Mayes, A. (eds) *Teaching and Learning in the Secondary School,* London: Routledge.

This chapter is a concise introduction to Gardner's work on multiple intelligences.

Bibliography

Bennett, N. and Dunne, E. (1994) 'How children learn: implications for practice', in Moon, B. and Shelton-Mayes, A. (eds) *Teaching and Learning in the Secondary School,* London: Routledge.

Claxton, G. (1984) *Live and Learn: An Introduction to the Psychology of Growth and Change in Everyday Life,* Buckingham: Open University Press.

Doherty, J. and Bailey, R. (2003) *Supporting Physical Development and Physical Education in the Early Years,* Buckingham: Open University Press.

Evans, J., Lopez, S., Duncan, M. and Evans, M. (1987) 'Some thoughts on the political and pedagogical implications of mixed sex groupings in the physical education curriculum', *British Journal of Educational Research* 13: 59–71.

Fitts, P. and Posner, M. (1979) *Human Performance,* Westwood, CT: Greenwood Press.

Gallahue, D. and Ozmun, J. (1998) *Understanding Motor Development,* New York: McGraw-Hill.

Gardner, H. (1994) 'The theory of multiple intelligences', in Moon, B. and Shelton-Mayes, A. (eds) *Teaching and Learning in the Secondary School,* London: Routledge.

Goleman, D. (1996) *Working with Emotional Intelligence,* New York: Bantam Books.

Granlees, J. Turner, I. and Trew, K. (1989) 'Teachers' and boys' and girls' perceptions of competence in the primary school: the importance of physical competence', *British Journal of Educational Psychology,* 58: 3–7.

Katene, W., Faulkner, G. and Reeves, C. (2000) 'The relationship between primary student teachers' exercise behaviour and their attitude to teaching physical education', *British Journal of Teaching Physical Education,* 31: 44–6.

Krechevsky, M. and Seidel, S. (1998) 'Minds at work: applying multiple intelligences in the classroom', in Sternberg, R. and Williams, W.L. (eds) *Intelligence, Instruction and Assessment: Theory into Practice,* New Jersey: Erlbaum Associates.

Laker, A. (2000) *Beyond the Boundaries of Physical Education: Educating Young People for Citizenship and Social Responsibility,* London: Routledge /Falmer.

Marsh, H.W. and Jackson, S.A. (1986) 'Multidimensional self-concepts: masculinity and femininity as a function of women's involvement in Athletics', *Sex Roles* 15 (7/8), 391–415.

Rich, E. (2003) 'The problem with girls; Liberal Feminism, "equal opportunities" and gender inequality in Physical Education, *Journal of Physical Education,* 34(1): 46–9.

Stewart, D. (1990) *The Right to Movement,* London: Falmer.

Sulliran, B. (ed.) (1996) *Teachers: A Tribute,* Kansas City: Andrews and Mcmeel.

Out of the Mouths and Minds of Babes: Language Acquisition and Development

Clare Holloway and Margaret Alfrey

Introduction

This chapter examines language acquisition and development and the crucial role of speaking and listening in children's understanding and learning. There are five main sections: (1) consideration of non-verbal and pre-verbal communication; (2) the place and value of non-verbal communication; (3) verbal communication; (4) some theoretical perspectives on children's language acquisition and development; and (5) the roles of carers and educators in the use of language as a tool for learning.

By the end of this chapter you should have:

- begun to evaluate the role of non-verbal and pre-verbal communication in the development of spoken language;
- gained some insight into the key processes of language development through an understanding of the various theories discussed;
- considered ways in which language skills are acquired;
- understood some of the links between language and learning.

You will have noted that we refer to 'carers' to include both parents and other adults.

Non-verbal and Pre-verbal communication

Although young children do not use words until about ten months to one year old, they use a very sophisticated non-verbal communication skill with their carers throughout that first year when their main concerns are to communicate and interact with them and other adults, and explore their social and physical environment. These interactions lay the foundation for spoken conversations.

Schaffer states there are two features which are essential characteristics of social interchange and these are: *reciprocity* and *intentionality*. Reciprocity refers to the child's understanding that an interaction needs to be participated in, and sustained by both speaker and listener. Intentionality is described as the 'ability to plan one's behaviour and anticipate its consequences ... it is also necessary for full participation in social interaction' (Schaffer 2002: 116).

At around eight months old the child begins to make specific demands. This means crying, and other cues, are used *intentionally* by the child to get what he wants or needs. For example, if a baby can see his bottle, he may cry to get the carer's attention and then look at the bottle and then back to the carer who construes the baby's intentions and offers the bottle. Of course, if the carer misconstrues the baby's intention and offers a nearby teddy, the baby will go on crying until he gets what he wants. Pre-verbal and non-verbal communication is clearly a two-way process with both baby and carer working together to address the baby's need.

O'Reilly (1997) sees the relationship between carers and young babies as an active interchange between two people who are each seeking to find out what the other is about. There is much research providing evidence of early interactions between adults and very young babies. Examples of this include carers smiling, followed by the baby smiling and the baby, responding to a sudden noise, looking at the carer with an 'Is it all right?' expression and relaxing when the carer makes reassuring noises.

As already mentioned, children tend not to use words until about ten months to one year old. According to Bruner (1983), the shift in use from non-verbal to verbal communication is promoted by the child's participation in what he terms *formats*. These are the routine turn-taking exchanges in games and other one-to-one interactions with a supportive adult. Bruner suggests that these *formats* provide the child with language-relevant understanding, or conversation-related skills, which may be drawn on when verbal communication is becoming possible.

An example of these one-to-one interactions with a supportive adult is in the turn-taking games carers often play with babies, as these tend to follow simple rules. The carer will talk to the baby, often asking him questions such as, 'Where's your blanket?', or 'Who's a beautiful baby?', she then pauses for the baby to respond. When the baby responds, whether it is with a smile, sound or gesture, the carer shows pleasure and this in turn leads to further interactions which encourage the baby to respond. Saxon (1997) emphasises this, writing, 'joint attention has been widely recognised as the interactional context of language learning', and, following a longitudinal study of mother–infant interactions and later language competence, reported that 'early joint attention plays some positive role in later language development'. One conclusion she draws is that this supports the Vygotskian perspective (to be discussed later) of the importance of the more experienced partner adjusting to the less experienced.

We can see from the above that the carer's role is crucial in enabling young children to find out what someone or something is about, in validating the child's words and actions through their interactions, and in sharing the child's view of the world in order to know where he is so as to build on his previous understanding.

Task 1

Observe an interaction between an adult and a child of between about four and ten months old. Note how the child communicates his needs, responds to the adult, or shows interest in things through non-verbal communication such as looking, pointing, or attempting to reach something. Consider how the adult responds at the beginning of the interaction, and tries to construe the child's intentions if his need is not initially apparent, and how the adult sustains and develops the interaction.

The place and value of non-verbal communication

Bancroft writes that languages are made up of symbols, which may be sounds or gestures that are arbitrary but must be used systematically. He goes on to say that, 'Given a system of this kind our own experience as users of language shows that language is capable of an indefinitely large range of expressions' (2001: 48).

In this section we will examine how gestures, or non-verbal dialogue, support and enhance our interactions. Non-verbal dialogue, sometimes called the silent sub-text, often emphasises understanding or emotion experienced by both speaker and listener. It also provides cues that may be missed out in speech, particularly between friends and family where dialogue is informal and can be fast moving. Such informal conversations often include hesitations, incomplete sentences, repetitions, and so on. When we know people well, we create, through familiarity and shared experience, words or gestures that may mimic people or represent an occasion, and these are frequently used as a substitute for accepted vocabulary and grammatical rules.

Children discussing a game of football in the playground provide an example of this:

'What a goal, d'ya see how it went?'
(*Child A runs around two friends and kicks, to represent the earlier shot.*)
'Yeah, but Beckham here set it up.'
(*Child B smiles and points to himself.*)
'Wasn't fair really, as the goalie was watching – you know – instead of the game.'
(*Child C inclines his head towards the sight of the headmaster approaching the group playing football.*)
'Yeah.'

These children have a shared understanding of the context, the people within it and the game being played. However, if we could not see the non-verbal accompaniments to the conversation – the silent sub-text – we may not have gained as much understanding of it.

The use of non-verbal interaction is universal and is used throughout our lives. We all use our hands and facial expressions when talking and listening, often without realising it. Some societies, such as those in South America, are particularly good at using gesticulation to accompany and develop the spoken word. They use gestures and signs which need no verbal input in order to be understood by other members of that community. For example, in Managua, Nicaragua, raising the first fingers from both hands and placing them side by side over your heart symbolises that you are talking about a girlfriend or boyfriend. A small change in movement so the fingers are moving alongside each other implies that the relationship is more advanced and pairs of lovers or a passionate relationship are being discussed.

In Britain, specific non-verbal greetings may be used to establish our roles in society and our relationship with those we meet. An illustration of this is that we curtsy or bow before the Queen, and kiss the hand of a religious leader. All of us use forms of non-verbal greeting which we deem suitable for various situations. Thus, even though the same verbal greeting of 'Hello' could be used for friend and foe, we may follow it up with a hug or kiss for those closest to us, kiss the cheek of friends, shake hands with colleagues or business acquaintances, and keep our bodies distanced and arms folded, or by our side, when encountering those with whom we are unfamiliar, distrust or dislike. Another example of non-verbal communication is when we are offered a chair by someone. Often the chair is indicated by a sweep of the hand or a nod of the head in the direction of the chair. A smile or a friendly glance can placate, reassure or put us at our ease, while in a meeting or shop, or at a bar, a direct look in our direction can assure us that we have not been overlooked and are included and noticed.

Task 2

Observe an informal conversation between two adults. Look at, and note, the facial expressions, gestures and body movements used to support and enhance the conversation.

In all the above examples it has been clear that, in any interaction and including those with silent sub-texts, there needs to be a listener and a speaker. We often say to children, 'Sit still, be quiet and listen.' Yet we all know children who are doing just that but have no knowledge or understanding of what has been said to them. Conversely, we know children who are apparently absorbed in another task and yet have complete knowledge of both what is going on around them and what has been said to them. Some of the learned reactions in our society, when listening to someone talk, are through our facial and body movements. We tend to look directly at the speaker, opening our eyes wide to encourage the speaker to continue. We nod to show we are following what is being said and frown or sharply take in a breath as if we are about to speak, or to signal that we are unsure of the speaker's meaning at this point. These facial and body movements reflect the meaning that the listener has constructed from the speaker. They are all forms of non-verbal communication and, as previously discussed, are similar to a carer's construction of meaning from non-verbal information given by the baby.

Task 3

Children are asked to listen for many purposes. These include listening for pleasure, for information, for instructions and for safety. Think of some examples of these. Also, consider the impact on children's communication that the classroom may have where there are one or two adults to 30 children. How might you support their speaking and listening skills in this context?

Verbal communication

Babies respond to speech at a very early age and at three to four months begin babbling and making sounds, and even though they may only hear English spoken, they produce sounds that are only heard in, say, an African language. These sounds eventually get dropped. Why is this? We might argue that carers particularly reward the sounds that are similar to those in their language by nodding, smiling, and repeating the sounds and responding less enthusiastically to those which do not approximate to their language. Equally, we might say that babies imitate the sounds they hear and keep repeating them when they are met with approbation. Another factor might be the consistency of the language input babies hear around them and the interactions with their carers and others.

Although young children's vocabulary increases rapidly, they appear to understand more words than they can produce. Eliot, examining language and the developing brain, reports:

> Between two and six, children are estimated to learn the meaning of a staggering eight words a day. That comes out to more than one new word every two hours they are awake, and they continue at this rate into elementary (primary) school years. By the time a child is six, it's been estimated that he understands some thirteen thousand words, although he doesn't speak nearly that many. (1999: 373)

As an example: a 22-month-old child when asked what was his favourite colour of car, picked up a yellow car and said, 'Yellow.' A few minutes later he picked up the same yellow car, and asked the carer, 'What yours?', indicating that he wanted to know her favourite colour car and understood the meaning of the word 'favourite'.

Children very quickly learn the names of important people, objects or events, such as mummy, daddy, drink, biscuit, bath, dog, car, and so on, and often take great delight in making animal and other noises at any time as if exploring the sounds they can make. Often this is used to quite considerable effect as they develop a sense of humour and begin to understand what is appropriate at certain times and what isn't!

Further, from a very early age, children learn to control their environment through language. They use one-word commands such as, 'up, more, go, bye bye' and that most frequently used word – 'NO'. In these ways they are not using single words merely to label but as a means to social interaction and control. They also use single words or sounds, such as 'da', to label, point, and demand or ask (as in 'What's that?'). Thus, a single word communicates much more than the word itself. Their ability to control their environment – and carers – continues when they begin to combine words. Common expressions are, 'no more, all gone, my car, more juice, do again, that not yours, that mine, mummy garden, that biscuit'. In these examples children are communicating actions, stating ownership and location, labelling, and recognising when something is no longer there.

Speech, then, becomes more and more important as a means of social interaction. However, the use of non-verbal communication continues. For example, a boy at around 18 months, pointed and said, 'More juice.' By two and a half years he was saying, 'I would like more juice', then, pointing, 'that juice, the yellow juice'. Then, noticing the cup picked up by the carer, went to the cupboard where the cups were, and said, 'I would like my car cup, not that cup.' At that stage the phrase, 'I would like' was in constant use, yet it was not a phrase he heard frequently. However, he had understood that by using it he was more likely to get what he wanted!

Some theoretical perspectives on language acquisition and development

Having considered children's early uses of language, we now need to consider some of the theoretical perspectives on how this tremendous achievement comes about and continues to develop.

During the late 1950s Naom Chomsky (1972) put forward the notion that all languages have the same basic structure of sentences, parts of speech, and rules about their use. He termed this 'Universal Grammar'. Because of this universality of language Chomsky proposed that all of us have innately what he termed as a 'Language Acquisition Device' (LAD). Since children create new words, for example a two and a half year old using 'peep' as the singular of 'people', he suggested that, 'language is constructed through grammatical rules that every human brain is programmed to discover, given just a few brief years of exposure' (Eliot 1999: 353).

Chomsky drew this conclusion as he believed it was not possible, from the language a child hears from his carer and others, to understand the complex rule systems of our language. Therefore, to learn such rules he must be born with some of the ability to recognise and use them. He supported his theory by pointing out that as children construct words they have never heard, such as *wented*, they also construct their own language rules. Alongside this, carers and other adults support the development and understanding of grammatical rules through their own use of spoken language, repetition and correction. For example, young children quickly learn that the past tense is usually formed by adding 'ed' and plurals by adding 's'. This may give rise to what at pre-school, but not at school, may been seen as amusing mistakes, such as the very common, 'I wented' and 'three blind mices'. This use of language should not be seen as a form of regression of understanding but as a sign that the child is grasping complex language rules. When children interpret the grammatical rules incorrectly, carers will correct them, providing the 'right' answer saying, when the child says, 'I wented to the park.' 'Yes you went to the park.' Children, over time, adjust their understanding and use of the past tense and plurals including understanding the exceptions to the rules.

Chomsky (1972) suggested that the exploration and manipulation of language slow up from the age of seven years. Therefore, although as adults our vocabulary continues to increase and develop, albeit at a much slower rate, we are less likely to take risks with language and stay within the confines of our experience and understanding. Thus when we learn another language in adolescence or adulthood, we tend to use it as taught, with little exploration or manipulation of the rules, and therefore our use of that language may be grammatically correct but rather stilted. For example, in our mother tongue we may ask, 'Got the time?' When speaking another language we would probably say, 'Would you tell me the time, please?'

As we have seen, put simplistically, Chomsky believes that language learning is innate whereas Vygotsky (1987) and Bruner (2001) stress that the vital factor in language acquisition and development is social interaction between the child and carer or other adult. Garton and Pratt (1990: 1) support this notion, arguing that the mastery of spoken language, reading and writing, are all dependent upon a supportive adult assisting the learner.

Piaget and Vygotsky (referred to in Chapter 1) differ in their views on the role of social interaction in children's development. Piaget considered that social interaction *merely* assisted the pattern of development of children's thinking, whereas Vygotsky asserted that social interaction *determined* it. In other words, for Vygotsky, the development of language begins with interaction between the child and carer. He focused on the role of instruction, seeing the educator extending children's learning by supporting, scaffolding and questioning, within what he described as the zone of proximal development (ZPD). Vygotsky's ZPD may be defined as the difference between what a child can achieve without help and what he can achieve with the support of an adult or peer. For example, a child randomly picking up pieces of a jigsaw and trying to fit them in may have his attention drawn, by the supporting adult, to the straight edges, or colour/shape matching. In other words, Vygotsky's notion of the ZPD may be thought of as the educator supporting the next step in the child's thinking of the task or problem in hand.

This has resonance with the work of Bruner who, as has been seen in Chapter 1, writes of the importance of the adult in scaffolding children's learning. The importance of social interaction is not only stressed by theorists and educators but also in the Cockcroft Report (1983). This Report highlighted the importance of the child talking through a mathematics problem before recording it. It reinforces the notion of the importance of social interaction in children's learning. As we saw in Chapter 1, children learn through active experience, through interaction with others, through talk (as a catalyst for learning) and through intervention in their learning threshold by carers and educators.

As adults we seek to find out what someone, or something, is about by accessing information in varied ways and drawing on our wide experience of the world. Children's main resource for finding out what someone or something is about is through talk and actions and the 'validation' of their experiences by the carer or other adults. In Vygotskyian terms, children direct themselves aloud by language and interaction to confirm understanding. For example, a six-year-old read, 'The tea clipper, *Cutty Sark*, won the blue riband that year'. (He was reading about tea clippers crossing the ocean to bring tea to Britain.) He re-read the passage and then spoke aloud as if to himself, 'Blue riband?' 'Is it like the channel ferries who get a blue ribbon for being the fastest?' He knew about the channel ferries as his father worked in the port of Dover. He then turned to the teacher for confirmation of his understanding, saying, 'The blue riband was given to the *Cutty Sark* for being the fastest tea clipper, wasn't it?' Tizard and Hughes (1984) would call this example a passage of intellectual search as the child was seeking to solve a problem and confirm his conclusion through internalising his thoughts (by voicing them aloud) and through interaction with a supportive adult.

Roles of carers and educators in the use of language as a tool for learning

As we have seen in an earlier section, various theories emphasise the importance of social interaction, and the role of a supportive adult in language acquisition and development. Obviously children come to school with a wealth of understanding and experience, and are certainly not beginners in literacy. They know a great deal about signs and symbols: what we might call environmental literacy. For example, they understand M for McDonald's, the symbols on the doors of toilets, even though the woman is often depicted as a triangle with a small circle on top, and that different coloured lights on traffic signals indicate when to stop and go. Children are also aware that saying, 'please', is more likely to get what they want and some are aware that you behave and speak differently in school to the way you speak and behave at home.

However, Wood (1998) and Donaldson (1986) suggest that children may find learning in school more difficult as our educational system depends greatly on abstract or disembedded (out of context) ways of thinking. Donaldson expands on this, saying that in school we may present tasks which do not arise out of the familiar and the purposes of which are not always clear. We sometimes use abstract, or out of context, instructions such as the well-known one in *Cider with Rosie* where the child comes to school and is told to 'sit there for the present' and by the end of the day complains to his mother that he sat where he was told but did not get a present! (Lee 1960). Donaldson believes children do not interpret words in isolation but try to interpret what the educator is doing, saying and may intend. Therefore what the educator does and intends are as important as her use of language.

Another difficulty which may arise when children come to school is that they do not appreciate that the educator does not have a shared understanding of their home experiences. Thus, if a child says, 'John, he's got a new car and it's like our granddad's, colour as well.' The carer will know that John is a friend who has a new toy car which is the same colour and make as granddad's. If the child reports this news in school, the educator does not have this shared background understanding and will neither know if John is an adult or child nor the colour or make of the grandfather's car.

Wood (1998) highlights two types of talk that occur when teaching children. The first of these is *contingency* in which the educator leads the child to further understanding through a series of verbal and non-verbal interactions that build on his previous experience and offers suggestions to encourage further exploration. For example, in preparation for a visit to the park, a young child may refer to a previous visit saying, 'Ducks in park.' The carer will expand this and follow with a question saying, 'Yes, that's right there are ducks in the park. Do you think they would like something to eat?' The carer will then lead the child through a series of questions to establish where the ducks are, what a suitable food for them is and how the food should be given. Wood's second type of language used in teaching is termed *control*. The carer or educator will tell the child what is going to happen at the park, saying, 'Yes, we'll go to the park and feed the ducks.' This response gives little opportunity to develop the interaction which would lead to finding out what the child already knows or extend his understanding.

Similarly, the use of questions (both open and closed) is a common tool to support children's learning. However, although both types of question are valuable, it is the open question that supports further development and understanding. For example, when reading a story, the educator may ask, 'What do you think will happen to the giant?' The response requires the child to demonstrate his ability to recall the story and predict, from the text and using his imagination, what is likely to happen to the giant. A closed question, such as 'What is the giant's name?' merely requires the child to recall given information.

Educators and carers can also support language and learning by reinforcing and repeating instructions by repeating the key segments of what the child is to do following the original instruction. For example, 'Will you get the new pencils please, they are on the bottom shelf in the red box, ... no the bottom shelf, ... in the red box.'

Task 4

Observe how an educator uses contingent language (guiding, supporting, providing opportunities for the child to offer suggestions and construct understanding) and controlling language (closed questions, directing children to a previously learned fact or how to complete a task). What difference do you think the use of contingent and controlling language might make to the child's learning and understanding of the topic?

One of the best-known tools for enhancing children's language development is the use of books. Eliot reports that, 'Two-year olds whose parents read to them early often show more advanced language skills than children read to less frequently, an advantage that seems to last well into the grade school (primary) years' (1999: 389). Educators and carers can, and do, use books to broaden vocabulary, introduce new concepts and ideas, stimulate imagination, conversation, and so on.

Another means of language enhancement in school is the use of cross-curricular or project work which involves children in learning new concepts and vocabulary, developing their listening skills as well as their spoken language as they explain, describe, hypothesise, debate and report their findings. Indeed, Hardman and Beverton (1993: 147) have shown that there is also a role for the interested and supportive adult in intervening and supporting children in the development of discussion skills. They state, 'Discussion strategies need to be explicitly taught through analysis and reflection, with pupils becoming aware of the roles that they can play in discussion, the suitability of those roles in different situations, and so on.'

Task 5

Read a book with children, noting the opportunities that arise for language enhancement and for them to demonstrate their understanding of the story.

Try to stimulate discussion at the end of the story and note children's awareness of their role in discussion.

Summary and key points

In this chapter we have discussed the relevance of non-verbal and pre-verbal communication in young children's concern to communicate with their carers and other adults as they explore their social and physical environment. This led to a consideration of the place and value of non-verbal communication and how it may support and enhance our understanding of interactions both in childhood and throughout our lives. Some theoretical perspectives were explored to try and explain the processes of language acquisition and development. These included an understanding of how children learn through experience; through interaction with other children and adults; through talk as a catalyst for learning and through the educator intervening at the child's learning threshold. The chapter concluded with a brief examination of the roles of carers and educators in the use of language as a tool for learning and their role in developing and extending children's ability to use all their language skills to enhance their learning.

Questions to aid reflection

1 What do you consider to be the main value of non-verbal and pre-verbal communication in the development of spoken language?
2 How might your understanding of some of the theoretical perspectives of language acquisition and development underpin your practice?
3 How has your understanding of the use of language as a tool for learning influenced you in your role as a carer and/or educator?

Annotated bibliography

Browne, A. (1996) *Developing Language and Literacy 3-8,* London: Paul Chapman. This book discusses how children learn, and apply, all aspects of language and literacy.

Lee, V. and Das Gupta, P. (eds) (2001) *Children's Cognitive and Language Development,* Milton Keynes: Open University Press. An accessible text covering children's development in a number of areas including mathematical and scientific thinking and development in reading.

Pinker, S. (1994) *The Language Instinct,* London: Penguin. Pinker discusses the Nativist view of language acquisition and draws on a variety of theories to support his arguments.

Wells, G. (1987) *The Meaning Makers,* London: Hodder and Stoughton. A comprehensive and readable text which examines the stages in children's language acquisition and development.

Bibliography

Bancroft, D. (2001) 'Language development', in Lee, V. and Das Gupta, P. (eds) *Children's Cognitive and Language Development*, Milton Keynes: Open University Press.

Bruner, J. (1983) *Children's Talk: Learning to Use Language*, Oxford: Oxford University Press.

Bruner, J. (2001) in Lee, V. and Das Gupta, P. (eds) *Children's Cognitive and Language Development*, Milton Keynes Open University Press.

Chomsky, N. (1972) *Language and Mind*, New York: Harcourt, Brace Jovanovich.

Cockcroft, W.H. (1983) *Mathematics Counts*, London: HMSO.

Donaldson, M. (1986) *Children's Minds*, 15th edn, London: Collins.

Eliot, L. (1999) *Early Intelligence*, London: Penguin Press.

Garton, A. and Pratt, C. (1990) *Learning to be Literate*, Oxford: Blackwell.

Hardman, F. and Beverton, S. (1993) 'Cooperative group work and the development of metadiscoursal skills', *Support for Learning*, 8, 146–50.

Lee, L. (1960) *Cider with Rosie*, London: Hogarth Press.

O'Reilly, J. (1997) 'The interplay between mothers and their children', in Bannister, D. (ed.) *New Perspectives in Personal Construct Theory*, London: Academic Press.

Schaffer, R. (2002) *Social Development* (9th edn) Oxford: Blackwell.

Saxon, T.F. (1997) 'A longitudinal study of mother–infant interaction and later competence', *First Language*, 17(51), 271–81.

Tizard, B. and Hughes, M. (1984) *Young Children Learning*, London: Collins.

Vygotsky, L. (1987) *Thought and Language*, New York: MIT Press.

Wood, D. (1998) 'Aspects of teaching and learning', in Woodhead, M., Faulkner, D. and Littleton, K. (eds) *Cultural Worlds of Early Childhood*, London: Routledge and Open University Press.

5 Children and Numeracy

Gina Donaldson, Claire Alfrey and Beryl Webber

Introduction

For many people, mathematics can be a daunting subject, some may even be intimidated by seeing it as an area which has never really been fathomable. Many people's feelings about mathematics stem from their early experiences at school, how they were taught mathematics, how they were encouraged to use mathematics and how the importance and relevance of mathematics was conveyed. The importance of giving young children a positive and confident approach to mathematics is vital. In this chapter you will be introduced to the development of mathematical knowledge and understanding in young children. Key issues in the teaching and learning of mathematics will be discussed, and you will be asked to reflect on your own use of mathematics in everyday life, and the way in which you learn mathematics most effectively. This should lead you to reach some principles of teaching and learning mathematics which will guide your further study and experience in school and encourage a positive and confident personal approach to mathematics. By the end of this chapter you should have:

- an introduction to some of the main theories of how children learn mathematics and how these may be applied in the classroom;
- an insight into the role of mathematical language in children's learning of the subject;
- a discussion of the role of problem solving and questioning in children's mathematical learning;

- an insight into the role of apparatus in the teaching and learning of mathematics
- an introduction to the philosophy and rationale of the National Numeracy Strategy (NNS);
- a discussion of the key issues relating to the teaching and learning of calculation strategies.

How do children learn mathematics?

Task 1

Reflect on your own learning of mathematics, whether at school, college or during individual study. What did you find most, and least, helpful?

- Have you had the experience of being taught by what you would describe as an effective teacher? What did he or she do? Did you learn through watching the teacher, or listening to the teacher, or did you discuss issues? Did you feel confident enough to speak when you did not understand, and to ask questions?
- Do you learn best through visual images, listening to explanations, or doing some practical work?
- What is an effective text book or worksheet? Have you ever worked on a written exercise which seems to be related to the mathematics which you use in everyday life? How much writing should be included on a worksheet?
- Reflect on your experiences of working with other people on mathematics. Do you feel that ability groupings, where you work with people of a similar ability, are supportive when learning mathematics? Is it ever useful to work in a mixed ability group? What are the benefits of each? What is the best size for a group? Have you ever worked in a pair?

Reflection on the times when your learning of mathematics has been most effective can help you to decide on a number of principles for the teaching and learning of mathematics. Look for similar features in experiences when your learning has been most successful, and note these down. As you continue to read, you will be able to add to these.

There are many theories which try to explain how children learn mathematics, and it is not easy to understand why some children appear to learn mathematics very quickly, while others find it more difficult.

Piaget and others have suggested that children do not learn passively, they need to be active participants. For example, children do not necessarily learn by listening to their teacher, they need to have practical hands-on experiences which enable them to construct knowledge themselves. Exploring the ways of making towers of 7 multilink with cubes of two colours can show that 1 + 6 is the same as 6 + 1, whereas being told that addition is commutative will not have the same impact. The teacher's role is to provide the necessary and relevant teaching, activities, resources and questions to support and scaffold the children's learning. The child is therefore working in what Vygotsky terms as their 'zone of proximal development' (for further details see Chapter 1), supported by the teacher in a way that enables the child's learning to be moved from the practical to the abstract. Further explanations of these ideas can be found in Nickson (2000), *Teaching and Learning Mathematics.*

Other writers suggest that it might be better to consider the learning of mathematics as the exploration of a spider's web of ideas and concepts which are interlinked. Skemp (1989) described effective learning of mathematics as relational rather than instrumental. He described this as finding your way around the roads in a city. If you are unfamiliar with the roads, you might have one route to get from A to B. If you follow this route, you know you will get there safely. However, if there is an accident, a diversion or if you accidentally take a wrong turning, you have no knowledge of any other road or route to take. Skemp described this as an instrumental understanding. You might have an instrumental understanding of division problems, for example. You may have one method of finding the answer, but if the problem does not relate easily to your one method, then you are left with no other strategy. If you are familiar with the roads in a city, you can take any diversion if there is an accident or a road is shut. You know exactly how the roads interconnect and can see the whole picture of the road network in your mind. Skemp described this as a relational understanding. If you have a relational understanding of mathematics, you are able to use a number of methods to find an answer, and you have some understanding of how these methods relate to each other. Therefore, if you are faced with a non-routine problem, you are equipped with many strategies, and the confidence these bring you to find a method to suit you.

This idea of learning mathematics as building up an understanding of the links and connections within mathematics is reinforced by the research of Askew *et al.* (1997). This research identified effective teachers as those who see mathematics as a web of interconnecting ideas and concepts. He calls this a connectionist view. Lessons are based upon the knowledge that the children already have in order to make connections to new ideas and concepts.

These teachers are aware themselves of the connections within mathematics and explore them with children within lessons. The following examples illustrate a connectionist approach.

- Connections are made between addition and subtraction, and multiplication and division.
- Fractions, decimals and percentages are all used to show varying ways of writing the same amount.
- A link is made between the different representations of mathematics by, for example, a teacher talking about addition and showing the children a tower of 3 multilink cubes and a tower of 4 cubes added together, while using the language of addition, and writing the symbols $3 + 4 = 7$ on the whiteboard. The connections between practical work, the language of mathematics and symbols are therefore reinforced.

All these examples draw upon the image of mathematics as a web of interconnecting ideas, with children learning by making connections to previous knowledge and experiences. A child who has made the connection between addition and subtraction is able to learn the addition facts up to 10, and therefore will know the subtraction facts. That is, if he knows $3 + 4 = 7$, then he also knows that $7 - 3 = 4$ and $7 - 4 = 3$. A child who has not learned this connection has to learn all three facts and commit them to memory. Therefore, a child who has not been taught this connection may actually be having to learn more mathematics, not necessarily with understanding, and may progress at a slower rate.

Task 2

Do you have knowledge of the connections within mathematics? Write the fact $4 + 5 = 9$ in the middle of a piece of paper, and write down around it all the ways of writing this fact, drawing it, explaining it and any other connecting fact.

　　Think back to your reflections on your own learning of mathematics and the teaching and learning of mathematics you have observed in school. Try to identify examples of connectionist teaching and learning.

The role of mathematical language in children's learning

'Language plays an essential part in the formulation and expression of mathematical ideas' Cockcroft (1982: 89). Language is the vehicle for communicating ideas and thoughts. Part of the problem with learning mathematics is that the written and spoken language is often abstract. For example, seven swans a-swimming has a meaning and can be visualised whereas '7' on its own cannot be visualised or defined without giving it a context. If you can put '7' into a context, it can be visualised and communicated. When children start to learn, they abstract from the physical world to create meaning. For example, they are given elephants to count and they will do this successfully. They will eventually internalise the principles of counting and the abstract nature of it and will not need the elephants to assist them. They will be able to re-contextualise their knowledge to any other counting situation. It is at this stage they can start to use mathematical language with meaning.

'Mathematics provides a means of communication which is powerful, concise and unambiguous' Cockcroft (1982: 1). But for those learning mathematics, is mathematical language unambiguous?

Mathematics has its own technical vocabulary just like any discipline such as geography, history, or music. Problems arise when words can have more than one meaning. The types of mathematical vocabulary can be categorised into three areas:

Ordinary English – table, odd, check
Mathematical English – number, sum, total, count
Technical Mathematical Language – scalene, isosceles, parallelogram.

Ordinary English

This area refers to specific mathematical vocabulary used in everyday language. Some examples of this type of language are number and half. Each of these words are used in everyday language and have more than one meaning, one of which is mathematical.

The National Numeracy Strategy (NNS) identifies the mathematical vocabulary required from the Foundation Stage to Key Stage 3. Many of the words are ordinary English words that take on a specific meaning in mathematics, for example, take away; is it a mathematical operation or a meal bought to eat at home?

Task 3

Identify ordinary English words that have a specific meaning in mathematics and a different meaning in everyday usage.

Word	Ordinary English meaning	How it is used in a mathematical context?
Odd	Out of the ordinary	A whole number which is not a multiple of 2

Observe and note any children using mathematical language and their understanding of the ordinary English usage and the mathematical meanings. Clemson and Clemson (1994: Chapter 5), discuss these issues further.

Mathematical English

This area of vocabulary refers to specific mathematical vocabulary used in everyday language but only with a mathematical meaning or context. Some examples of this type of language are number and half.

Technical mathematical language

This area of vocabulary has a specific mathematical meaning and is not used out of a mathematical context, such as scalene and isosceles where referring to types of triangles.

Mathematical language and the classroom

Use of mathematical language by adults

In order for any adult to be able to ensure that children are familiar and confident with their understanding and use of mathematical language, they need to be knowledgeable and confident themselves to introduce and use the words in a relevant and meaningful context. This can be done in a number of ways:

- Planning for mathematical talk – within any lesson or group planning, an adult working with the children needs to be aware of the correct mathematical vocabulary associated with the concept/skill/knowledge being taught. In addition, the language will need to be contextualised in a way that is meaningful for the children.
- Giving examples – for children to develop a full understanding of what

the word capacity means, a whole range of containers should be provided for the children to explore.

- Questioning – adults can intervene in a constructive way. Questions should be open to help and develop children's thinking and ability to discuss.
- Use of words in displays – displays of children's mathematical work could include relevant vocabulary. A specific mathematical word board could be provided which allows children to see the words written down and choose a word to define the meaning.
- Use of mathematical dictionaries – for personal use by the adult and child to help define terms.
- Providing an enabling environment to support children's mathematical discussion in a confident and non-threatening manner – this will need organisational considerations and a positive ethos within the learning setting.

Task 4

In a child's learning environment observe and note down how mathematical language is introduced and used by adults.

Children's use of mathematical language

Children need to become confident in the use and understanding of mathematical vocabulary if they are to understand mathematical concepts, skills and knowledge. They can be supported in a number of ways:

- Communicating thoughts – being encouraged to communicate thinking within peer group discussion, for example, 'How did you work that out?
- Clarifying ideas – children need to be encouraged to discuss their emerging thoughts and ideas in order to refine their understanding and draw generalisations. For example, I know that 4 x 3 is 12 and I understand the principles of doubling, so if I want to get 8 sets of 3 I know I have to double 12.
- Reflecting on their own and others' ideas – within any activity children need to be encouraged to reflect on their own ideas and those of others, how ideas and methodologies are similar, how they differ and which may be the best to use. In discussing different methods, children will be able to appreciate other ways of working and adapt their own thinking and understanding where necessary.
- Posing their own questions – children should be provided with opportunities to pose their own questions, rather than simply answering the questions of someone else. This applies very much to problem-solving situations which are discussed in more detail later.

- Finding solutions – children should be encouraged to 'have a go' at any mathematical problem. The ethos of the learning environment should be such that the child feels confident enough to offer solutions that may differ from those of other pupils working in the same group. Many problems in mathematics can have more than one solution; often children are fixed on the idea that mathematics is only about giving one right answer. For example, the answer to my question is 48, what might my question have been?

Language is fundamental to mathematics and needs not only to be taught, but also to be well defined by the adult working with the children and understood and verbalised by the learner.

The role of problem solving and questioning in mathematics

Problem solving is fundamental to mathematics. It is woven into the National Curriculum and is one of the five strands of the National Numeracy Strategy. What is problem solving in mathematics? There are three elements: making decisions; reasoning; and solving problems.

Making decisions

When problem solving, you will make many decisions about how to tackle the problem, which mathematical operations to use, and which resources you might need to help you. It is necessary to be able to read the text of the problem and make sense of it. The next stage is to extract the mathematics from the text and decide on the method of attack. This involves many skills such as those set out below:

- thinking skills
- information-processing skills
- enquiry skills
- creative thinking skills
- reasoning skills
- evaluation skills
- communication skills.

Reasoning

Reasoning is about generating patterns and solutions to problems and puzzles. When tackling a problem, you might make a general statement about a mathematical pattern. You should be able to explain your thinking about numbers and shapes in words, pictures or symbols. The teacher or another adult can support the development of reasoning by asking open-ended questions through which learners are able to explain their working and also increase their enquiry skills.

The most important question in teaching and learning mathematics is 'why?'

- Why does the rule work?
- Why must the next number in the pattern be odd?
- Why do these shapes fit together?
- Why is a square a special type of rectangle?
- Why do we use digital and analogue measures of time?
- Why do we need to prove things in mathematics?
- Why do we learn mathematics?

Learners can be encouraged to become mathematical thinkers by the use of questions that challenge perceptions and encourage the learner to move into higher order thinking.

- What would happen if ...?
- Does it always happen?
- What is the pattern?
- How can we solve this another way?
- What is number?
- What is mathematics?
- Why do we need algebra?
- When do we apply algebra in our everyday lives?
- Is there another solution?
- In how many ways can we solve this problem?

Solving problems

For many adults, problem solving in their mathematical education was about the rate that men dug holes! However, it is now recognised that problem solving is a life skill (Thompson 1999) and will have more meaning and usefulness if taught in a real-life context.

Solving problems is about allowing children to think for themselves. In practical terms this often only means turning a closed question such as 'How much is 15p add 20p?' into 'What coins could be used to buy two items costing 15p and 20p?' This again demonstrates the need to make mathematics meaningful.

Task 5

Thinking back over the past few days, what mathematics have you used to help you solve a problem?

The role of apparatus in the teaching and learning of mathematics

Before children start school and encounter formal mathematics, they have been observing mathematics in use and using mathematics themselves. Young children and their carers can often be heard counting the numbers of steps they are going up or down. Many nursery rhymes such as 'one, two buckle my shoe' and 'five little speckled frogs' encourage not only familiarisation with numbers but also number sequences. Everyday activities such as the sorting of socks and shoes into pairs, the counting of plates to people at tea time, use of language such as 'before lunch', 'tea time' and 'bed time', all introduce a variety of mathematical concepts to children. It is through these experiences that 'very young children are able to begin to develop mathematical understanding' (Edwards 1998: 8).

If young children gain valuable insight and understanding into mathematical concepts through practical experience, so too can older children. Mathematics teaching will be more formal in schools than the informal learning children may have experienced at home, however, practical experience will be a part of children's learning and it will be supported by the use of practical resources. The National Numeracy Strategy in its Framework for Teaching Mathematics (DfEE 1999a: 29) actually outlines what resources it feels should be in classrooms (the resources depend on the age of the children in the classroom). Examples are given below:

- a long number line
- a 'washing line' of numbers
- number tracks
- digit cards
- place value cards
- addition and subtraction cards
- symbol cards
- 100 square
- small apparatus such as counters multilink, pegs/pegboards
- squared paper
- number games, measuring equipment, sets of shapes and construction kits
- books on mathematics

- story books which support mathematical concepts such as *Then the Doorbell Rang* by Pat Hutchins
- mathematical dictionaries.

In a Foundation Stage classroom there should be a good range of play resources, outside and inside, which allow adult- and child-initiated play. Examples include: balls, hoops, skittles, beads, sets of animals, board games and tea-sets.

Such resources and apparatus should be used in mathematics lessons to build a link between the concrete and the abstract nature of mathematics. The use of apparatus in itself will not, however, teach the children these links, it is the teacher who will allow the children to make the connections in the lessons and through the activities they plan and deliver. However, it is through using such resources and apparatus that the children reinforce and consolidate knowledge gained. Children may be very comfortable in the use of concrete materials to carry out basic counting, then move onto counting using their fingers as an interim method but 'the aim is for children to become less reliant on fingers and apparatus and to calculate mentally' (DfEE 1999a: 30). However, children will only move on in their understanding when they are ready. Resources can be used, as Bruner suggests, to 'scaffold' children's learning in that they embody the mathematics that the children are learning (for further details, see Chapter 1). For example, place value cards can be manipulated by children to explore place value and challenge the misconception that twenty-six is written as it is said, that is, 206.

Whatever the age of a child, they can benefit from using apparatus in mathematics lessons. If you think how you learn best, it may well be through doing or through experimenting. Thus, a child can be supported in his learning through careful selection of, and appropriate use of, apparatus which may help a child move from the concrete understanding of a mathematical concept to an abstract understanding.

The National Numeracy Strategy

The National Numeracy Strategy was introduced in 1999 as a means of raising standards in mathematics in the primary phase. It closely followed the Third International Mathematics and Science Study (Harries *et al.* 1997) which published the results of a series of tests undertaken by children in various countries across the world. This study showed that children here performed very poorly, particularly in areas such as understanding of number, when compared with the rest of the world. Researchers then looked at the way in which mathematics is taught in countries where children appeared to perform much better than those in this country, with a view to sharing this good practice. As a consequence, the National Numeracy Strategy includes many ideas which can be traced back, for example, to whole-class teaching in the Pacific Rim countries and an emphasis on mental calculation in countries such as Hungary and the Netherlands. Although it is not easy to take teaching styles and practices which work in one country, which may have a particular culture, and transplant them to another country, the National Numeracy Strategy has been widely welcomed by teachers.

The National Numeracy Strategy aimed to raise standards through the following:

- a dedicated mathematics lesson every day;
- direct teaching and interactive oral work with the whole class and groups;
- an emphasis on mental calculation;
- controlled differentiation, with all pupils engaged in mathematics relating to a common theme.

(DfEE 1999a: Section 1:11)

You may feel that the term numeracy refers to number aspects of mathematics only. The National Numeracy Strategy defines the term numeracy in the following way:

> Numeracy is a proficiency which involves confidence and competence with numbers and measures. It requires an understanding of the number system, a repertoire of computational skills, and an inclination and ability to solve number problems in a variety of contexts. Numeracy also demands practical understanding of the ways in which information is gathered by counting and measuring, and is presented in graphs, diagrams, charts and tables.
>
> (DfEE 1999a: Section 1:4)

Clearly this definition of numeracy includes much more than the understanding of number, which is how the term may have been defined before the publication of the National Numeracy Strategy. The NNS includes shape, space, measures, problem solving and data handling.

Task 6

Reflect on your observations of mathematics lessons in school. Consider one or two effective lessons or parts of lessons. Do these lessons contain any of the features you identified as useful in your own learning?

Look for lessons which include visual images, listening activities and practical work. Do the children have a range of activities during a week's worth of lessons? Which activities seem to be most effective?

Are the children able to ask questions and say when they do not understand? Do they discuss issues with their teacher or teaching assistant?

Try to establish the objectives for a lesson before you observe it, and ask one or two children about the area of mathematics to be covered beforehand. Assess whether they already have any knowledge or understanding before the lesson. Question them again after the lesson to consider what they have learned. Then reflect on how the learning took place.

The Strategy suggests the use of a three-part lesson. However, this is to be used flexibly to meet the needs of the children, and the learning objectives of the lesson. The lesson usually takes the form of a mental and oral starter (5–10 minutes), direct interactive teaching (5–15 minutes), group, paired or individual work (10–25 minutes) and plenary (5–15 minutes).

Key issues relating to teaching children calculation strategies

Task 7

What sorts of calculations do you use in your everyday life? This might have been while shopping, laying the table, driving, carrying out some DIY or programming the video. Have you done these in your head, on paper or on a calculator? You may have used a mixture of methods. Do you use methods you were taught in school, or ones you have developed yourself?

The National Curriculum and the National Numeracy Strategy place a great emphasis on children's mental strategies. You may remember mental arithmetic at school yourself, and many people's experience of this was a series of mental arithmetic tests. The approach of the NNS is to help children to develop a range of mental strategies, and an appreciation of which strategy is best fitted for which problem, rather than simply testing them.

For example, how would you calculate 7 + 8? Many of us would have this as a known fact and be able to say immediately that 7 + 8 = 15. Children might use a bridging method where they are familiar with the addition facts to 10 and so know that 7 + 3 = 10, leaving 5 more of the 8, so 10 + 5 = 15. This can be shown on a number line.

Eventually, given enough practice in games and mental and oral starters this would become a known fact which could then be used say to calculate, say, 17 + 18.

How would you calculate 25 + 32? Many of us would use a partitioning strategy, saying 20 + 30 = 50 and 5 + 2 = 7 so 50 + 7 = 57. Or we may say 25 + 30 = 55, and 55 + 2 = 57. Here we are using knowledge of place value. However, there are many other strategies. If the numbers were closer together, say, 28 + 29, we might work this out by using our knowledge of doubles. We might know that double 28 is 56, so 28 + 29 = 57. It would be inappropriate for children to be solving 28 + 29 by counting on in ones on their fingers. This would be an ineffective method. Unless children are introduced to other methods though, they will continue to count on in ones.

Mental strategies, of course, happen in the head, and it can be difficult to teach and assess strategies where there is little evidence of what is being thought. One way of teaching a class a new strategy is for the teacher, or one of the children, to model the strategy, and to describe it, and the rest of the children to try and use the method to solve a similar problem. However, we know that many children do not learn effectively purely by listening. Therefore the empty number line can be a very good visual model to help children to describe the strategies they are using and learn about new ones. For example, the teacher may have one child in the class who uses a compensation method to add 99, and wish to teach this to other children. For example, he may solve 27 + 99 by 27 + 100 − 1. In the lesson, the teacher might draw this on the empty number line.

This visual image can be very effective alongside the teacher's explanation. Mental calculations do not have to take place purely in the head. Sometimes it is very useful to make jottings on paper to assist more complex calculations.

Details of which facts children should have as rapid recall, and which mental calculation strategies should be taught to each year group can be found in the National Numeracy Strategy and the QCA booklet (1999b) *Teaching Mental Calculation Strategies*. Thompson (1999) *Issues in Teaching Numeracy in Primary Schools* includes chapters on the teaching of mental calculations and the use of the empty number line.

In the past, standard written methods of calculations have been taught to children as early as Key Stage 1. These are the compact methods which are usually arranged vertically and which split the numbers up into digits, and deal with one column at a time. For example, the standard written method for addition often looks like this:

```
  5 6 4
+ 3 2 9
  8 9 3
    1
```

Children find these methods quite difficult to learn, as they are contracted, and rely on a secure understanding of place value. Many errors occur when the children have not fully understood why the method works, and therefore try instead to remember how it works. This represents a significant burden on the memory, and once a step is forgotten the children have no understanding of what to do next.

The National Numeracy Strategy suggests delaying the introduction of these written methods until the children have secure mental methods, and a good understanding of place value. It is important nevertheless that they are introduced to children, as they are very powerful methods, particularly useful for very large numbers and for numbers with several digits after the decimal point which could not be easily tackled mentally. The QCA booklet (1999b), *Teaching Written Calculations*, gives a very useful progression for introducing these standard methods to children.

The National Numeracy Strategy states that whenever children have a problem to solve, they should firstly try to do it mentally. If they are not able to find a solution in their heads, then they should use paper and pencil, and if this is not possible they should use a calculator. Therefore, children have to be taught about the sorts of problems which are best solved with a calculator and how to use a calculator effectively. The Strategy provides support material and ideas for activities for teachers to do this.

Summary and key points

Some of you may have begun reading this chapter with trepidation. The issues discussed should have challenged your preconceptions about learning mathematics. Today's teaching of mathematics will be different to many of your personal recollections and experiences. There is very much an emphasis on a dynamic interactive learning environment which stimulates the learner and incorporates good use of relevant resources and equipment. Mathematics should stimulate curiosity. Problem solving, and asking challenging questions, are ways of creating a mathematically stimulated learner who appreciates that mathematics is useful in all contexts, not just something that happens in the classroom.

We have addressed some of the main theories of how children learn mathematics and how these may be applied in the classroom. Reflecting on your own mathematics may help you to recognise and understand these theories. Educators' own understanding and use of mathematical language enable children to engage with mathematical discussion and use the correct terminology in a relevant context. The NNS offers a framework for the teaching of mathematics within which language plays a central part. It provides a structured approach to the teaching and learning of calculations and emphasises the need for flexible and effective mental and written calculation strategies.

If all these strategies are implemented, children will approach mathematics with a positive and confident attitude and appreciate the relevance and fascination that the subject can hold.

Questions to aid reflection

1 Reflect on a mathematics lesson you have seen taught, to what extent did the teacher use the following to enhance teaching and learning?
   - making connections
   - use of mathematical language
   - focus on problem solving
   - use of questioning
   - use of apparatus.
2 Reflect on your own mathematical education. What were the factors which made your teachers most effective? Did you experience teaching which was of a connectionist nature?
3 When has your own learning been most effective? What are the implications of this for your own teaching of mathematics?

Annotated bibliography

Askew, M. (1998) *Teaching Primary Mathematics,* London: Hodder and Stoughton. A guide to the teaching of each area of mathematics throughout the primary phase.

Atkinson, S. (ed.) (1992) *Mathematics with Reason,* London: Hodder and Stoughton. A discussion of informal and formal mathematical understanding.

Clemson, D. and Clemson, W. (1994) *Mathematics in the Early Years*, London: Routledge. Covering teaching and learning in the first three years of school. Discusses a range of issues.

Haylock, D. (1995) *Mathematics Explained for Primary Teachers*, London: Paul Chapman Publishing Company. A book which explains mathematics subject knowledge, sets problems for the reader and provides the answers.

Montague-Smith, A. (1997) *Mathematics in Nursery Education*, London: David Fulton Publishers. A book which outlines young children's mathematical development and learning in a variety of strands of mathematics.

Bibliography

Askew, M., Brown, M., Rhodes, V., William, D. and Johnson, D. (1997) *Effective Teachers of Numeracy: Report of a Study Carried out for the Teacher Training Agency,* London: King's College, University of London.

Clemson, D. and Clemson, W. (1994) *Mathematics in the Early Years*, London: Routledge.

Cockcroft, W.H. (1982) *Mathematics Counts*, London: HMSO.

DfEE (1999a) *The National Numeracy Strategy,* London: HMSO.

DfEE (1999b) *Mathematical Vocabulary*, London: HMSO.

Edwards, S. (1998) *Managing Effective Teaching of Mathematics 3-8*, London: Paul Chapman Publishing.

Harries, S., Keys, W. and Fernandes, C. (1997) *Third International Mathematics and Science Study, Second National Report Part 1,* Slough: National Foundation for Educational Research.

Nickson, M. (2000) *Teaching and Learning Mathematics*, London: Cassell.

QCA (1999a) *Teaching Written Calculation*, London: QCA.

QCA (1999b) *Teaching Mental Calculation Strategies*, London: QCA.

Skemp, R. (1989) *Mathematics in the Primary School*, London: Routledge.

Thompson, I. (ed.) (1999) *Issues in Teaching Numeracy in Primary Schools*, Buckingham: Open University Press.

An Introduction to Science and Technology

Helen Conder and Kevin Ward

Introduction

This chapter suggests ways of thinking about science and technology in a range of learning environments, the role that learning theories have in how children learn the content of the science and technology curriculum and other issues which impact on how they learn this subject knowledge. This chapter will *not* give you an introduction to scientific concepts and knowledge; plenty of texts provide this in a straightforward manner. We hope that you will begin to examine and question the role, content, and place that these subjects have had at the centre of the curriculum and whether this centrality is justified.

By the end of this chapter you should have:

- an understanding of the science and technology curriculum for England and Wales;
- developed an understanding of how children and young people acquire skills and knowledge in science and technology;
- an understanding of how various attitudes influence learning in science and technology.

The science and technology curriculum

This section provides an analysis of the nature of the science and technology curriculum from the Foundation Stage through Key Stages 1 to 4.

The purpose and nature of the science and technology curriculum

What is science? What is technology? Why do educationalists consider these areas to be an important part of the school curriculum? We are concerned about what these curriculum areas mean to you and children in an educational setting so we will avoid a complex philosophical discussion here. In the context of your workplace, consider your own view of each of these curriculum areas.

The National Curriculum for England and Wales (DfEE 1999) outlines the science and technology curriculum for all pupils at Key Stages 1 to 4, and the Foundation Stage (QCA 2000) outlines the content for young children in the early years setting.

Defining the nature of science in school is no small task. For the benefit of simplicity, we will view science in schools as a body of explanatory knowledge and attitudes relating to concepts and models developed from repeated experimentation from initial hypotheses. The National Curriculum itself is split into four distinct areas:

Sc1 – Scientific Enquiry – concerned with the process by which learners carry out their scientific investigations and acquire the body of knowledge. This is explored further later.

Sc2 – Life Processes and Living Things – mainly concerned with the 'biological' aspects of science.

Sc3 – Materials and their Properties – mainly concerned with the 'chemistry' aspects.

Sc4 – Physical Processes – mainly concerned with 'physics' aspects.

Design and Technology (D&T) may incorporate some aspects of what was formerly the craft subjects in earlier curricula but the emphasis within 'D&T' will focus on design and making, using the 'design process' to guide the development of solutions to either a given design problem or one that pupils have formulated themselves. Pupils will develop their ideas from the observation of a context (for example, 'how to improve the school's playground facilities') or by choosing their own context to observe, through to evaluating their final practical outcome (for example, a scale model of a redesigned play area). It is the two- or three-dimensional outcome that the learner produces that sets this curriculum area apart from science. The focus for educators is to promote what is termed design and technology 'capability' among learners. Morely (2002) shows the relationships between the various 'capability' components (Figure 6.1) and relates this to an everyday process (Figure 6.2).

Pupils will use a variety of materials in their work. More traditional

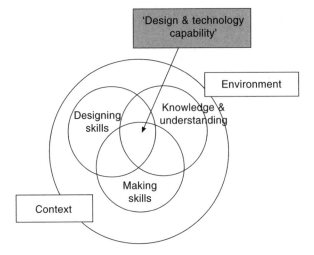

Figure 6.1   Design and technology capability
Source: Morely 2002

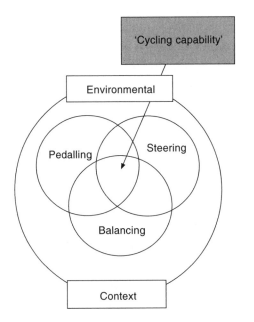

Figure 6.2   Cycling capability
Source: Morely 2002

materials will include wood, metals, plastics, graphic products, electronic and pneumatic components, and food and textiles materials.

Within the early years, *Curriculum Guidance for the Foundation Stage* (QCA 2000) contains a specific area of learning, called 'knowledge and understanding of the world'. This guidance helps to structure the experiences that young children bring from their life within the home to their first educational experiences at nursery or a similar experience.

Organisation of the curriculum

How this curriculum content is managed in schools is less straightforward. At Key Stages 3 and 4 there is a fairly well-established system of departments and faculties within schools that have the responsibility to deliver the National Curriculum content for these areas. At Key Stages 1 and 2 the boundaries between science and technology can be blurred or non-existent. At the Foundation Stage these subjects are integrated within all areas of learning. A number of models of delivery are apparent; from total integration with a single subject coordinator, to total separation with separate subject co-ordinators for each area. A full evaluation of these approaches is not the purpose of this chapter, but readers are invited to consider the practice in their workplace in Task 1.

Links between the two areas can be grouped into philosophical (those relating to the nature of activities undertaken) and practical (those relating to the logistical and practical considerations). Links between two subject areas in secondary schools are few, although there is the potential to share common ground. This has led to researchers such as Barlex and Pitt (1999) suggesting that much more could be done to ensure a complementary approach at Key Stages 3 and 4. Their research showed that there were indeed few links, not only within schools but also by few concrete links within the National Curriculum documentation itself. The report highlights P. Gardner's (1994) four models regarding the relationship of science to technology:

1 'Technology as applied science' – Science precedes technology therefore technological capability grows through applying scientific knowledge.
2 The 'demarcationist' view – Science and technology are totally independent, with different methods goals and outcomes.
3 The 'materialist' view – Technology precedes science.
4 The 'interactionist' view – Science and technology inform and challenge each other. Neither area is seen as dominant.

It is argued that within the secondary curriculum, especially with the lack of cross-over within the National Curriculum documentation, that a demarcationist view is dominant. Barlex and Pitt (1999) noted that while a variety of views were held regarding the four models outlined above, most felt that a demarcationist view was undesirable. In Task 1 we ask you to consider which view is the dominant one held in your workplace. A variety of initiatives could be introduced to lessen the divide between the two areas, but at the very least this has implications for staffing and timetabling, as well as a necessity for two groups of educators to become more knowledgeable about each other.

With design and technology no longer a compulsory foundation subject within the National Curriculum, educators who judge it to be valuable will have to fight their corner even more effectively to ensure the position of this subject is not eroded further, especially within the primary curriculum.

Task 1

Consider the management of science and technology in your workplace. If you work with the early years children, how do the activities undertaken by the children fit the requirements of the 'Early Learning Goals'? If you work within the primary phase, how is science and technology delivered and co-ordinated in your workplace? Does a combined approach cause problems in covering the curriculum? How aren't the two curriculum areas linked in the secondary school (or are they?). If they are not, can you ascertain what is prohibiting closer links? Does the *interactionist* or *demarcationist* view prevail?

Theories of development and processes by which learners develop skills, knowledge and understanding in science and technology

The first chapter in this book will have introduced you to the ways in which children learn and to the work of Piaget, Vygotsky and Bruner. In the further reading of this chapter the work of Hodson and Hodson (1998) will provide you with an accessible introduction to these theorists and their theories as they relate to learning in science.

A constructivist view of learning as an active process transports us far from the idea that people are 'empty vessels' waiting to be filled with knowledge and understanding. If we are continuously and actively building our knowledge and understanding, then we are developing scientific ideas about the world around us from the moment of birth. We use these ideas to explain what we see and what happens to us, as well as forming the basis for our expectations and predictions. As Johnston (1996) suggests, the concepts we develop about our environment occur as a result of our experiences and exploration. We can predict, for example, that the sun will come up tomorrow, based on the prior observation that the sun goes down each day and comes up again in the morning. Yet, just as the earliest explorers travelled to the 'edge' of the world to see if it really was flat, so when our ideas or theories cannot be tested satisfactorily against our accumulated experiences, then we must test them empirically, that is go out and collect more evidence (Qualter 1996).

In the same way that we might describe science as a body of theories or ideas which are tentative in nature and which are replaced with new and better theories as understanding grows, we could also describe the development of young people's learning in science as a gradual development of understanding.

Children's learning in science or changes in scientific thinking will be determined by the quality of their experiences, which in turn are influenced by their cultural background. For example, some British research has shown that when learners were asked to explain how they determined whether certain objects were alive or not, most learners mentioned movement and growth as factors. However, when similar questions were asked of Buddhist school children in Nepal, the most common responses related to whether or not something breathes (Hanson and Qualter 1995; cited by Qualter 1996). The responses in both samples were fairly accurate in classifying living and non-living things, but the reasons for these answers were different.

Naturally, young people's concepts about their world will develop regardless of whether these 'experiences' are similar or different to others or whether they are helpful, or unhelpful, towards developing sound scientific understanding. With the plethora of emotional, social and cultural influences on scientific learning and understanding there is, inevitably, plenty of opportunity for confusion, ambiguity and misconception to arise. Later in this section we explore some of these misconceptions and we will consider ways of building learners' understanding and changing their ideas towards a more scientific view. First, we look at the skills, attitudes and values, with which we can support learners' development in order to encourage the processing of their ideas and information in science and technology.

Process Skills

Laying foundations for later learning and for helping learners to understand the world around them is an important reason for teaching science and technology from an early age. Children's ongoing and later understanding should be supported by the skills, ideas and attitudes we help them to develop. The way in which we encourage learners to process their ideas and information and their attitudes towards using these skills can be described through a 'processed-based' model where scientific processes such as exploration, observation, asking questions and trying things out are central features. This model describes skills which are common to science and design technology.

For younger learners in particular, 'doing' is intimately bound up with 'knowing' and these two elements should not be separated. We could consider that the younger the child, the more emphasis we should place on the procedural (doing) aspect, in comparison with the conceptual (understanding) components of scientific learning. If we consider, as suggested by Davies and Howe (2003), that young learners, 'think' with their hands, we recognise that their learning is 'profoundly kinaesthetic' and that we need to provide opportunities for experiences with materials, whereby they can be directly involved and develop their manipulative and cognitive capabilities. There are differences between the two 'fields' of course and many would consider that design technology has more in common with art and design than it does with science. Consider, for example, some of the government schemes of work for design and technology which involve making, say, slippers or musical instruments. While there are different purposes for these activities, learners, as scientists, seek to understand the world as it is, while design technologists seek to make practical changes. Although there is some variation in the way these processes are described by writers, the skills and attitudes are common components of any investigative activity. Here we generally use Harlen's (2000) clarification and identification of the terms for scientific skills:

- raising questions;
- developing hypotheses;
- making predictions;
- gathering evidence: planning;
- gathering evidence: observing;
- interpreting evidence and drawing conclusions;
- communicating and reflecting.

Closely associated with the ability to use these skills is the willingness to use them (Harlen 2000). Therefore it is also important to develop values and attitudes of curiosity, flexibility in thinking, respect for evidence, sensitivity towards the environment and critical reflection. These values will be briefly discussed later, but for now we will look more closely at the individual process skills and consider what they mean in practice.

Raising questions

Raising questions in the context of science is raising questions which can be investigated, for example: 'Why do crisps come in bags?' or 'Do microbes grow in sub-zero temperatures?' These are science-related questions, different to opinion-type questions, for example: 'Which is the most delicious biscuit?' Such questions require value judgements. 'Science-related questions' require answers through investigation, or by asking someone who has already discovered an answer. Encouraging learners to raise questions of this nature means asking questions which lead to enquiry and helping them to recognise the sorts of questions that can be answered in this way.

Developing hypotheses

If scientific theories are tentative, then we can see that part of scientific enquiry involves considering more than one possible explanation, for example, 'the warmer the water, the faster the sugar dissolves'. A hypothesis is a process where an idea found to explain things in one context can be applied to another situation.

Making predictions

Predictions are closely related to hypotheses. For example, the prediction that 'a cup of hot tea will taste sweeter than a cup of cold water after a spoonful of sugar is added to both' will include the hypothesis that sugar dissolves more quickly in warmer water. Predicting is not guessing. A prediction, as well as a hypothesis, has a rational basis in an idea or in observations.

Gathering evidence: planning

A child may gather evidence from a variety of sources. Sources may include the materials they are working with, as well as secondary sources such as books, the Internet, classmates and adults. It is likely that plans for their inquiry will develop from consideration of such evidence. It is likely that unanticipated events will occur and that, in the light of these, plans will need to change frequently. Once the situation is set up, then gathering evidence via observations or measurement can begin.

Gathering evidence: observing

This aspect of the process involves more than just 'looking' or 'taking in' information gathered by the senses. A preconceived idea, or expectation, will influence what is seen. This can be useful for a focused approach but can also mean that useful 'evidence' is missed.

Interpreting evidence and drawing conclusions

The learner will use the findings or evidence to answer the questions that the investigation sets out to deal with. This interpretation might involve recognising a pattern or trend, piecing together fragments of information which tell more when they form part of a whole than when they are viewed separately, and relating the results to an idea on which the original prediction was based.

Communicating and reflecting

It is often through explaining things to others that we begin to examine them and understand them more clearly ourselves. There are various forms of communicating information and it is important to select the appropriate form depending on the type of information and the audience receiving it. Information can be communicated, for example, through speech, drawing, writing, objects, tables or diagrams. Communication is, of course, about receiving as well as explaining details, and involves the senses such as listening and looking to gather information.

Process skills in design and technology

In contrast to the investigative inquiry-type nature of science activities, most activities within Design and Technology will focus on design and making by using a 'design process' such as Kimbell's as a guide (see Figure 6.3).

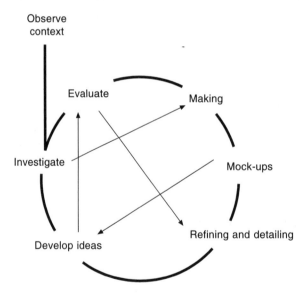

Figure 6.3 The circular design process model
Source: Kimbell *et al.* 1987

You will notice similarities between the science and design technology models. In both procedures the learner is reflecting on and evaluating their findings or outcomes in the light of their initial questions or ideas. During the design process, in particular, the various steps are opportunities for the learner to look back to previous stages of the design and to review progress and make changes and amendments as the project develops.

Learners in the design process will develop their ideas from observation of a context, and expand these through to evaluating their final practical outcome. For example, let us consider the 'slippers' project mentioned earlier. Influenced by the learner's observations and investigation of a selection of types of slippers, the original design brief or idea might identify the need for the final product to be, for example, 'pointed' or 'warm'. Throughout the process the learner will need to be addressing how he or she is going to achieve this specification. Finally, the learner will need to evaluate how far the final product (the slippers) meets their original specification. For example: Are they pointed/warm? How closely do they meet the original idea? What influenced the final outcome? It is this two or three-dimensional outcome that really sets design technology apart from science.

Developing values and attitudes

Proficiency and confidence in the use of the scientific and design processes are important for successful development in these fields. Nonetheless, we might consider that more influential in the development of skills and understanding, in any field, is the individual's emotional disposition towards learning. Later in this chapter we explore factors influencing the learner's approach to science, but here we briefly consider attitudes within science. In science and design technology, the learner's responses to phenomena act as openings to developing, for example, open-mindedness, curiosity, respect for evidence, flexible thinking, critical reflection and sensitivity in investigating the environment. These approaches, crucial in both fields of activity, are identifiable as scientific *attitudes*.

Such attitudes, Harlen (2000) considers, are not taught but 'caught', for they exist in the way people behave. Learners will 'catch' these attitudes through example and by approval of behaviour that reflects the attitude. In developing process skills themselves, learners will also be fostering a general approach beneficial to developing scientific attitudes. Skills and attitudes, which are common to design and technology and science, can be fostered through examples given by the teacher, opportunities for attitudes to be shown and reinforced, making allowances for individual differences and providing time. Some of the practical strategies and approaches that can be employed to develop such scientific attitudes will be explored later in this section. Since space is limited in this introductory text we recommend Harlen (2000) and Johnston (1996) to the reader for more specific details and definitions of scientific attitudes.

Having discussed the processes by which children and young people develop skills, knowledge and understanding in the areas of science and technology, let us now turn to some of the misconceptions and alternative frameworks that learners hold in relation to language, ideas and thinking in science. Such misconceptions can influence the attitudes of the learner and the extent to which they develop scientific understanding and 'scientific literacy'.

Language and ambiguities

Language plays a vital role in the development of ideas. Communication must involve the shared understanding of words and their appropriate usage, whether the words and their meanings are 'scientific' or 'everyday'. Our use and interpretation of language for everyday or scientific purposes give rise to numerous confusions and obscurities and unless the teaching adult is vigilant, ambiguities in thinking and understanding occur. Take, for example, the introduction of the term 'volume' to a group of six and seven year olds. This created initial confusion during an investigation involving measurements. Most of the learners associated the term with sound on the TV, or their CD player, and did not relate the term to the measurement of space. In another situation where children were talking about 'temperature', it became obvious to the adult that the learners were making connections with situations where people are unwell. To have a 'temperature' was perceived to be undesirable. The learners were not associating temperature with a general measurement of the hotness of something, but with something that a person had if they were sick and did not have if they were well. Other words such as 'scales', 'conductor' and perhaps even 'coolest', which have scientific and everyday meanings, are among many potentially confusing terms used in science. No doubt the reader can think of other examples of ambiguities, or confusions, which they have witnessed first hand.

Task 2

Record a scientifically based discussion from your workplace and make notes on any important or scientific vocabulary used or any vocabulary misused. What are the implications for learners' understanding of the issues or concepts under discussion?

Scientific concepts and ambiguities

Further ambiguity is highlighted in work carried out by Rix and Boyle (1995) where learners demonstrated alternative meanings for everyday words which, it had been taken for granted, needed no further explanations to make their meaning explicit. For example, a child identified the sun as being 'alive'. This learner had heard from somewhere that 'the sun never dies'. Logically he had concluded then that if it 'never dies', then it must be alive. It is not difficult to understand how a common vagueness in use of the term 'alive' could lead to uncertainty and misconception. Pupils' ideas about 'heat' indicate that younger children tended to associate heat with living objects, sources of heat, or the degree of hotness of an object, while older children also associate heat with objects but also with energy. It is interesting that, despite having been 'taught' this area of science, older pupils still associate 'heat' with meanings they had constructed in their day-to-day experiences of hot and cold objects. Educators need to be aware of the fact that such explanations can become a basic part of a learner's own explanatory framework when similar problems are encountered in a school setting.

If our learners are working with personal alternative frameworks, while developing their scientific language, understanding and views and these 'frameworks' are not reconstructed towards a more scientific view, then it is not difficult to envisage the multitude of confusing ideas and misconceptions that could ensue. How, then, can we help learners develop a clearer understanding of scientific concepts and support them in applying these ideas in real life as well as in scientific contexts? Let us explore some of the effective ways of supporting young people's learning in science via teaching attitudes, models of practice and useful materials.

Developing supportive environments and attitudes

Opportunities for the learner to develop scientific attitudes will be determined largely by the general views of the supporting adults and the learning environment created. If the learning context sustains and encourages curiosity, exploration and questioning in all circumstances, then enquiry, collaboration, tolerance, flexibility, sensitivity, critical reflection and creativity are more likely to ensue.

Asking questions and challenging ideas

A learning environment where open questioning, sharing of ideas, discussion, enquiry and critical analysis are part of the every-day climate is likely to be a setting where alternative frameworks can be explored and challenged and where the learner's thinking can be extended.

Questioning is fundamental in science and design technology. Human knowledge has been extended through asking questions though, of course, not all questions are asked for scientific reasons. For example, questions may be asked to obtain information, assess learning or understanding, control behaviour or extend thinking. Some observers in schools have found that teachers' questions, usually related to management, dominated classroom questioning and gave little opportunity for pupils' questions. Being able to ask questions which frame the appropriate learning outcome is crucial to extending children's thinking and will rely very much on the knowledge and confidence of the educator or questioner. Children's progress in scientific understanding is, in turn, reliant on these effective questions (Feasey 1998).

Effective questioning: open or closed?

How can we encourage effective questioning and thinking in the classroom? As already suggested, confidence to ask questions develops with knowledge and understanding in an area. The more we know, the more questions we tend to ask. For young learners, confidence in asking questions and giving answers is also engendered by the way in which their questions and responses are received and valued.

If questions require only single or limited replies, for example: 'How many legs are there on the chair?' or 'What colour is the chair?', only a small number of individuals will be able to participate before the 'correct' answer is reached. While such closed questions will help with familiarity of the chair, the range of responses will be limited. Open questions such as 'Why do you think the chair is that colour?' encourage a variety of responses which extend thinking and raise opportunities for further design-type questions and exploration. Learners will recognise that their responses are of value and will feel encouraged to contribute.

The supporting adult's use of open-type questions will provide a useful model for children developing their own questioning skills. Increasing opportunity for asking questions through, for example, brainstorming, interactive display, question boxes, interviews and 'think books', will encourage children to become confident and successful questioners.

Learners challenging and reconstructing their thinking

Learners will not change their ideas or views simply because they are told a more scientific alternative. For example, if you learned here for the first time that when dropped from the same height, an apple and a screwed-up sheet of paper will hit the ground at the same time, would you alter your original ideas? When you need a break from studying, go and try it for yourself!

If there is no alternative idea available that makes sense to a child, there is unlikely to be a turnaround in his thinking. For example, during a topic on growth, a group of ten year olds were confident in their predictions that seedlings would not grow in a dark cupboard. The children had 'learned' that plants needed light to grow during their science lessons in Key Stage 1.

Imagine their confusion and amazement when they collected the pot after four days and discovered that the plants had grown to three or four times their original height. This was not what they had expected! Plenty of discussion ensued and although pupils noted that the plants were thin and 'leggy', they were still equating increased height with successful growth. It seems that although direct experience is undoubtedly a powerful way to learn, our ideas, once established, are not easy to alter. A child's turnaround in scientific thinking may require some strong and convincing alternative experiences with equally strong support from adults or peers to 'scaffold' his progression.

If reconstructing the learner's understanding of scientific concepts is necessary for developing a more scientific view, how can we introduce alternative scientific views without undermining the learner's confidence in his own thinking and interpretation? In the environment of a 'questioning' classroom there will be opportunity for discussion and sharing of ideas. Hearing ideas which differ from their own will encourage learners to consider alternatives, to question and to challenge. When their own views are challenged, children will be more prepared to produce evidence and arguments to support their thinking. Introducing a range of viable alternatives such as those in *Concept Cartoons*, Naylor and Keogh (1996), is a way of providing more scientific ideas. These 'cartoons' provide several plausible alternatives to a particular scientific concept. Learners can adopt or dispute the given alternatives and there is plenty of opportunity for dialogue which can explore thinking, prior knowledge and understanding. Children's ideas and the thinking behind them can be investigated and, as Feasey (1998) suggests, this can offer a 'window' into these ideas. Many of the ideas can be tested out practically and they offer opportunities for peer tutoring and challenging which are most powerful and effective in promoting conceptual change and developing children's ideas. In short, the cartoons are an effective resource for challenging and developing the scientific thinking of children *and* adults.

Information and Communication Technology (ICT) in science and technology

Although developments in ICT have had major repercussions in many curriculum areas, perhaps the most significant have been the changes within design and technology. These changes have been at the root of the development of the subject itself: a move away from the practical, skills-based approach of 'craft studies' to embracing the computer-controlled language of industry and commerce. This has meant for some educators a difficult transition away from years of accepted practice and the development of new skills.

Within science the most significant use of ICT has been 'data logging'.

This uses a 'peripheral' (a device that plugs into a computer and is controlled by it) that can, for example, sense and record temperature. This allows learners directly to input results of an investigation into a computer, or a hand-held device, which will then show the output, if required, in the form of a table or graph.

Using ICT within design and technology is divided into three main areas: (1) designing and making; (2) modelling; and (3) controlling. Many learners will also use standard word-processing, desk-top publishing, database and spreadsheet programs. We are interested in those that are particular to science and technology. The use of the CD-ROM as a reference tool has its place in this work and the more useful programs will enable interaction and contribute to the creative process. An example of this would be using a CD-ROM of materials and their properties to determine the best material for the manufacture of a product.

The creative nature of design and technology enables the use of ICT as part of the designing and making process. There is need at this stage to become familiar with more acronyms. The two most common are CAD (Computer Aided Design) and CAM (Computer Aided Manufacture). The two are often seen together (CAD/CAM) as you may use CAD to design an object and then, instead of printing, you will download to a machine that will *make* what you have designed (CAM).

There are occasions in the learning environment when the ability to be able to 'model' a situation can be useful. This may be because of the cost of components, materials or the lack of an expensive piece of equipment. An example could be the use of a program such as 'Crocodile Clips' to model an electronic circuit before the learner embarks on constructing the circuit with real electronic components.

Many examples of 'control' technology can be found in the home. This helps makes the concepts directly relevant to learners. The washing machine is a commonly used example. A programmable chip is used to store the various functions of the machine that is set into operation by the user. Control technology is now an integral part of the National Curriculum and various packages are available which allow programs to be written to control many types of peripherals, such as a multidirectional buggy. A newer development has been the introduction of a 'PIC' chip (Peripheral Interface Controller) whereby a program is written and then downloaded onto a computer chip. The chip can be used in may different types of projects (alarm systems and remote buggies are common examples) which do not have to be linked to a PC.

It should be noted that all of the above examples use ICT as an interactive part of the learning process. A passive use of ICT with little focus, such as using the Internet for 'research', has limited benefit to the learner.

So why use ICT in these curriculum areas? The standard justification for the use of new technologies has been the need to mirror developments in industry. However, there is a major difference between industry and education in the process of design and manufacture. Industry will want to produce multiple copies of a product and it therefore makes economic sense to use ICT to replicate the product many times. In education we will rarely want to produce more than a 'prototype', usually meaning one example. So a simpler rationale would be the need to expose the learner to the role that new technologies have in industry. A cynical response would be that the National Curriculum demands its use, leaving us with no choice.

Criticisms of using ICT revolve around the learner not needing to develop those skills that ICT can now provide. For example, a CAD program such as 'ProDesktop' will produce a three-dimensional image from a two-dimensional drawing. It will 'render' it (add colour and a visual interpretation of texture) and let you view the object from multiple angles. This takes away the need to teach young people the various three-dimensional drawing conventions, or does it? Most educators will tread a middle course and start with drawings on paper so that the basic concepts can be taught and understood before moving to apply them using a PC. Another cause for concern is that educational contexts lag behind industry. What is cutting edge in education is usually no longer current in industry. Combine this with the complexity in use of most industry standard CAD/CAM programs and we can see that a compromise is inevitable.

The arguments for and against the use of ICT in science and technology are largely academic. In general we know that learners enjoy using ICT in their work. Whether or not it promotes cognitive development is debatable; there is a lack of longitudinal research in this area. What we do know is that the use of new technologies is here to stay. With government investment set to continue, we should look at the practical issues of supporting these developments in science and technology – especially in the area of staff development – which will allow the confident *and creative* use of ICT in our teaching.

Task 3

How is ICT used in science and/or technology in your workplace? Is there a policy in place that promotes their use? What prevents ICT from being used more widely? Investigate any staff development issues. Audit the types of programs, hardware and peripherals in use. Begin to evaluate their effectiveness in use. What are the learner's views of using ICT?

Attitudes in science and technology

There are complex issues surrounding gender, transition and relevance of the curriculum to learners. A whole chapter in this book has been devoted to gender and we would ask that you transfer the ideas you encounter there to the situation in science. As these areas are complex, you are encouraged to consult the references to develop your own opinions and perhaps consider views and opinions that may question what you currently believe. All these issues have a wider relevance to the debate on the educational experience of children and young people. Are these curriculum areas relevant to children and young people? What are the tensions between providing specialist scientific training and a more general curriculum providing 'scientific literacy'?

Task 4

Ask a group of children to draw 'a scientist'. Be careful about the language you use which should not be gender- or job-specific and be careful not to provide examples – it will cloud their perceptions! Analyse the pictures. Are there any common traits that children define a scientist as having? Did the children have any difficulty with the concept of what 'a scientist' was or did? Try to engage them in a discussion to follow up any questions that the activity has raised.

Summary and key points

This chapter should be viewed very much as a basic introduction to the issues raised. The importance of questioning why and how children learn in science and technology has been outlined. You are encouraged to check publications and websites for up-to-date information on current research trends in these subject areas. In helping children understand science and technology we have seen how constructivists show that we develop ideas from our own social, emotional and cultural influences and experiences. There are strong links between the scientific process and the design process. Process skills, attitudes, and the creation of a learning environment that is supportive of an exchange of ideas through, for example, enquiry, questioning and discussion combine to develop positive 'scientific attitudes'. Such 'attitudes' can be usefully applied across all areas of learning. We can use ICT to data log, design, make, model and control in science and technology. Considering any development in ICT is difficult without 'hands-on' experience so try to observe and try out some subject specific software and hardware!

The relevance of the science curriculum has been questioned. The debate surrounding education's role in providing scientific 'experts', or a requirement to provide a common ground of scientific and technological understanding has been outlined.

Questions to aid reflection

1 What are the critical factors influencing a learner's development of scientific understanding?
2 What opportunities are provided in your workplace for supporting learners and young people working towards a 'scientific view'?
3 Reflecting on the issues raised in this chapter, consider your own attitudes towards the areas of science and technology. What are the main influences on your thinking? To what extent have your own early learning experiences contributed to these views?

Annotated bibliography

Feasey, R. (1998) 'Effective questioning in science', in Sherrington, R. (ed.) *ASE Guide to Primary Science Education*, Cheltenham: Stanley Thornes Ltd (for the Association for Science Education).
   This chapter discusses the importance of effective questioning in developing children's understanding in science. The vital role of the 'questioner' in this process and their own confidence, knowledge and understanding in science is highlighted. A discussion of the different types of questions we can ask and some useful strategies to encourage questions are presented.
Harlen, W. (2000) *Teaching Learning and Assessing Science 5–12*, 3rd edn. London: Paul Chapman Publishing.
   This is a seminal text for all those interested in science education. Much of the content is also applicable for those in the secondary phase. An approachable introduction to how children learn in science.
Hodson, D. and Hodson, J. (1998) 'From constructivism to social constructivism: a Vygotskian perspective on teaching and learning in science', *School Science Review*, 79(289), 33–41.
   This journal article provides an accessible introduction to both constructivist and socio-constructivist theories and the role that both Piaget and Vygotsky have in developing perspectives on how children think and learn. A second article was published (volume 80, number 290) which explores the area further.
Sears, J. and Sorensen, P. (eds) (2000) *Issues in Science Teaching,* London: RoutledgeFalmer.

A number of contemporary issues that affect the teaching and learning of pupils in science are explored.

Journals

Educational journals are essential to provide up-to-date research and information on issues relating to education. The *School Science Review* and *Primary Science Review* (both published by the Association for Science Education) offer a variety of articles on both practical science issues and theoretical perspectives on the areas covered in this chapter. The *Journal of the Design and Technology Association* provides a useful resource for those focusing on design and technology in school.

Web resources

The following web resources will help your introduction to the areas of science and technology:

AstraZeneca Science Teaching Trust
http://www.azteachscience.co.uk/

This website carries a number of professional development units on areas such as concept cartoons, effective displays, concept mapping and questioning in science. Follow the units on-line or download them to your own computer.

Crocodile Technology
http://www.crocodile-clips.com/index.htm

This is a popular modelling program that incorporates modules for science as well as design and technology. The website offers a free 30-day demonstration.

Design and Technology Association (DATA)
http://www.data.org.uk/welcome/welcome.htm

Homepage of the support network for design and technology. There are many resources from health and safety to curriculum initiatives.

DfES Standards site
http://www.standards.dfes.gov.uk/schemes/

Downloadable schemes of work for science and technology, useful for seeing how the National Curriculum can be turned into lessons

Education-Line
http://brs.leeds.ac.uk/~beiwww/beid.html

Based at the University of Leeds and forming part of the British Education Index, this site 'provides an internet medium through which authors can present early versions of their work and interested parties can keep abreast of topical issues in educational research'. There are many articles relating to both science and technology education issues.

Nuffield Foundation – 21st Century Science
http://www.21stcenturyscience.org/home/

Homepage of the group empowered with developing a relevant Key Stage 4 examination course.

Bibliography

Barlex, D. and Pitt, J. (1999) *Interaction: The Relationship between Science and Design and Technology in the Secondary School Curriculum,* London: The Engineering Council.

Davies, D. and Howe, A. (2003) *Teaching Science and Design and Technology in the Early Years*, London: David Fulton Publishers.

DfEE (1999) *The National Curriculum*, London: HMSO.

Feasey, R. (1998) 'Effective questioning in science', in Sherrington, R. (ed.) *ASE Guide to Primary Science Education*. Cheltenham: Stanley Thornes Ltd for the Association for Science Education, pp.156–67.

Gardner, H. (1983) *Frames of Mind: The Theory of Multiple Intelligences,* London: Collins.

Gardner, P. (1994) 'Representations of the relationship between science and technology in the curriculum', *Studies in Science Education*, 24: 29–47.

Hanson, D. and Qualter, A. (1995) 'Nepali children's understanding of "alive"', *Primary Science Review,* 38: 26–8.

Harlen, W. (2000) *Teaching, Learning and Assessing Science 5–12*, 3rd edn, London: Paul Chapman Publishing.

Hodson, D. and Hodson, J. (1998) 'From constructivism to social constructivism: a Vygotskian perspective on teaching and learning in science', *School Science Review*, 79(289), 33–41.

Johnston, J. (1996) *Exploring Primary Science and Technology: Early Explorations in Science*, Buckingham: Open University Press.

Kimbell, R. *et al.* (1987) *Design and Technological Activity: A Framework for Assessment,* London: HMSO.

Morely, J. (2002) 'How can we meet the challenges proposed by a new model of practical scholarship?', in Sayers, S., Morely, J. and Barnes, B. (eds) *Issues in Design and Technology Teaching,* London: Routledge Falmer.

Naylor, S. and Keogh, B. (1996) *Concept Cartoons in Science Education,* Sandbach: Millgate House.

QCA (2000) *Curriculum Guidance for the Foundation Stage,* London: QCA.

Qualter, A. (1996*) Exploring Primary Science and Technology: Differentiated Primary Science,* Buckingham: Open University Press.

Rix, C. and Boyle, M. (1995) 'I think I know what you mean', *Primary Science Review,* 37: 19–21.

'Mind the Gap': Creativity and Learning

Derek Greenstreet and Steve Varley

Introduction

Modern living demands flexibility and adaptability in thinking and learning due to the rapidity of change in so many walks of life. To cope with challenge and pace of this kind, children need to develop creative and imaginative ways of thinking, learning and acting to prepare them for their adult lives, for work and also for their free time. This clearly has implications for educators in planning and organizing learning opportunity in the classroom. This chapter will give an overview of the place and value of creativity in the development and learning of children, focusing on the way in which the learning environment gives opportunity for children to respond to their world in different ways. The impact of those who contribute to the process of children's learning will be examined. We will consider how early experience should be given continuity and progression in the curriculum. A further dimension will be the role of schools in providing curriculum opportunities conducive to creative teaching and learning. Readers will be encouraged to examine a range of literature and their personal experiences and to relate these to current practice in education.

By the end of this chapter you should have:

- developed an understanding of creativity and implications for the curriculum;
- understood the need to observe children in a range of contexts in order to identify modes of response to a full range of learning experiences;
- examined the links between early creative opportunities and a curriculum which is conducive to different teaching approaches and varied learning outcomes;

- considered the contexts in which creative learning takes place and its contribution to the full curriculum.

Understanding creativity

Creativity is thought of as being constructive, productive behaviour that can be seen as action or accomplishment.

(Lowenfeld and Brittain 1975: 61)

The term creativity is used very liberally to describe a range of human activity that is often far removed from being a 'creative act'. The word 'creative' too readily precedes inappropriate areas of experience, implying a misunderstanding of what the term actually means. We have recently come across a recipe book which suggested being creative with fish, a DIY magazine advocating being creative with paving slabs and an insurance brochure detailing 'creative' approaches to home insurance! In school too we use the word over-generously by, for example, making reference to creative writing when the framework given is set by the teacher, allowing very little creative thought or experience. In contrast, we seldom use the word in connection with science, mathematics or technology, implying that these do not allow for creative interpretation or exploration. Clearly, this undervalues the potential of teaching creatively across the curriculum.

A second important point is that creativity is characteristically linked with imagination. In some contexts they are viewed as being the same thing. This adds further complexity to the task of attempting to define both creativity and imagination. It is right to think of them as being linked, with the one feeding the other; being creative frequently requires a considerable element of imagination. While imagination concerns the formation of images in the mind, which do not exist, creativity is the process by which such images become reality.

Educators need to be clear about how creativity and imagination are, by definition, different, but equally are linked and often work hand in hand. To provide a single, all-embracing definition of creativity and imagination is probably impossible. We will therefore consider each in turn, to clarify our thinking and steer us towards ways of developing creativity and imagination in the classroom.

The *Concise Oxford Dictionary* defines creativity as 'bringing into existence', whereas the *Collins English Dictionary* adds the words 'imaginative or inventive'. We come to the awareness that creativity and output cannot easily be divorced from each other. They are closely intertwined and, as such, provide a particular way of learning which is informed and visionary. 'Creativity is not merely the capacity for certain kinds of "productive" action – it is the quality of being, a mode of cognition. Creativity can be nurtured, can be reinforced, and can be recovered' (Ross 1978: 14).

All our Futures (NACCCE 1999) made a strong case for creative approaches to teaching and learning in the classroom. The following quotation provides, not a definition of creativity, but a clear description of how it functions and how necessary it is for creativity to be nurtured and promoted.

> There are many misconceptions about creativity. Some people associate creative teaching with a lack of discipline in Education. Others see creative ability as the preserve of the gifted few, rather than of the many; others associate it only with the arts. In our view, creativity is possible in all areas of human activity and all young people and adults have creative capacities. Developing these capacities involves a balance between teaching skills and understanding, and promoting the freedom to innovate and take risks.
>
> (NACCCE 2000: 4)

There are salient messages for both educators and learners in this quotation. First, the implication that creativity is a process. Children develop creative abilities through the practical application of thoughts and ideas. The process begins with the 'rough shaping' of an idea, followed by a review of the original idea and a consideration of a range of possible alternatives. This part of the process leads to the elimination and refining of the range of possibilities down to a focus of one main idea to be developed. Often this is not the original idea. The final stage includes giving attention to detail to ensure that all aspects of the eventual outcome have been considered and necessary changes made. Second, the quotation confirms the premise that creativity is present in all human experience making creative capacity to be within everyone's grasp, provided that it is nurtured and grounded in a climate of creative and imaginative experience. Third, it promotes the view that creativity is potentially present in all areas of human activity. The implication is that the classroom must be a place to offer children the opportunity to develop their creative capacities at whatever stage of physical and intellectual development they have reached.

Imagination differs from creativity by definition in that it rests more with the formation of images in the mind rather than more formalised thoughts and ideas. The *Concise Oxford Dictionary* defines imagination as 'a mental faculty, forming images of external objects not present in the senses'. The reference to the senses is worthy of consideration. While all children, and particularly the youngest, rely heavily upon their senses to give meaning to early learning experience, the facility to develop and enrich the use of imagination takes them into realms beyond the real and tangible, into the world of fantasy and the unreal.

We constantly encourage children to 'use their imaginations' but are then often guilty of not allowing this to happen. We may even become quite negative by accusing them of making 'silly' responses or not thinking. Imagination allows children to become 'free agents', to visit new and unknown territory, activating mental behaviours that can be applied to enrich learning experience. Out of what might be seen to be 'mental chaos' comes order and meaning of a kind that triggers the creative process.

Duffy (1998: 19) states that to imagine is to do the following:

- detach oneself from the tangible world and move beyond concrete situations;
- not be restricted to the immediate perceived world;
- internalise perceptions;
- separate action and objects from their meaning in the real world and give them new meanings;
- bring together and integrate experiences and perceptions;
- contemplate what is not but might be; to pretend.

This implies an encounter with fantasy and the unreal; imagination frequently, but not entirely, has little to do with the real world. Children are enabled through using imagination to acquire 'sensible meaning' without depending on real, external influences. Duffy (*ibid.*) further reminds us that children are not always being creative simply because they are using their imaginations. Imaginative response can be quite repetitive, a means of simply repeating known roles and situations. However, imagination gives children the opportunity to visualise in their minds what does not exist; creativity can help them to convert what they visualise into reality. Creativity brings imagination to fruition.

Characteristics of creativity

Being creative requires something more than merely following rules or conventional practice. Yet being creative is not merely subjective. It is not sufficient merely to be divergent or different in any way whatsoever. It requires being different in a way that counts as appropriate.

(Best 1983: 27)

Every child is born creative (Lowenfeld and Brittain 1975: 63). The desire to explore, experiment, investigate, to satisfy curiosity, to make and create is a natural driving force. The classroom should be one place where such activity is encouraged and fostered. While all children possess a creative dimension, to a greater or lesser extent, some demonstrate particular characteristics in their approach to learning, in the way they assimilate knowledge and apply it to different situations and circumstances. These characteristics need to be identified and accommodated in the classroom for learning potential to flourish. Definitions of creativity are extremely diverse. No one definition can adequately encapsulate what the process of 'being creative' involves or how it will manifest itself within the classroom. Therefore we need to be aware of particular characteristics of creativity in order to assist children to become 'creative learners', providing an environment conducive to individual approaches to learning. Some learn through visual means, while others assume a more auditory approach, with others relying on a purely kinaesthetic stance (Jacobson 1983; Gardner 1984). The presence of creativity is not represented by set learning behaviours but rather by a series of possible and probable traits that determine patterns of learning. In addition, creative children frequently display behaviours that reveal ways in which they prefer to function that may help teachers to identify and meet their particular needs. Typically creative children:

- prefer to work independently, as opposed to collaboratively, in order to make their own judgements and decisions. They seldom seek the opinion of other children or even the teacher;
- frequently contribute the most ideas when given the opportunity which accords with their tendency to be divergent thinkers;
- are almost always the most resourceful children, particularly in challenging and less than straightforward situations;
- are usually able to justify their decisions and actions, particularly when faced with criticism or opposition;
- generally remain undaunted, when faced with complex or difficult tasks, revelling in the opportunity to meet the challenge and find a solution.

It should, however, be noted that many children who show creative and imaginative tendencies may not always be the cleverest children when judged against 'normal' classroom assessment criteria. Educators therefore need to monitor how children approach the learning tasks they encounter, observing those who demonstrate a number of the characteristics defined in order to meet their needs as learners. To undervalue the role of creativity and imagination in learning is to deny children the chance to enhance a vital dimension of their overall development, forming links and making connections between one set of ideas and another.

Creativity has sometimes, quite wrongly, been thought of as being related solely to arts-based activities such as drawing, painting, music, drama and dance. While such activities engage the creative dimension of human life, it can equally be found in and applied to other areas of learning such as the mathematical, scientific and technological areas. Some might argue that there is an even greater need for creative scientists, mathematicians and economists than there is for artists, musicians and poets. For mankind to continue to develop and progress we need to ensure that the creative faculty is kindled in all children who will in turn carry a creative approach to learning through to adulthood, thus providing a more creative workforce and contributing to an improved world economy.

The Arts in Schools (Calouste Gulbenkian Foundation 1982: 10–12) suggests that creative and imaginative experience gives children the opportunity to do the following:

- develop the full variety of human intelligence;
- develop the ability for creative thought and action;
- nurture feelings and sensibilities;
- explore values;
- understand cultural change and differences;
- develop physical and perceptual skills.

The opportunity to develop fully and extend these precepts has been allowed to decrease. By shifting the emphasis away from measuring, testing and assessing more towards enriched learning and 'hands on' experience, we will allow children to become more flexible and adaptable in their approach to learning. This is not to imply that creativity or creative processes cannot be assessed or that learning cannot benefit from close monitoring. It does, however, draw our attention to embracing opportunities for meeting the challenges of the adult world.

Creative children frequently question what is required of them, preferring to explore their own routes around a task rather than the one presented to them. Consider this observation of an art lesson with a Year 4 class. The children had been given the task of painting a single flower bloom, held in a small vase, on each of their group tables. The teacher had provided a thoughtful introduction to the lesson, encouraging the children to observe closely the shape, colour and texture of the petals, leaves and stem and to think carefully about how they would achieve close colour mixing and matching in order to represent the flower. Towards the end of the lesson the teacher berated one boy who, rather than producing a painting of one single flower bloom, had scanned the room and painted a spray of flowers, with considerable skill and technical precision. It was by far the most creative piece of work produced. The teacher's view, however, was that he had not listened or done what he had been asked to do. His view of things, his creative abilities and achievement were devalued, as he had not met the 'set' requirement.

Creativity manifests itself in a variety of ways, not following any set pattern or routine. It is possible, therefore, for teachers to misinterpret creative approaches to learning, as displayed by some children, as a negative response to their teaching. Creative children may be viewed as a nuisance, potential troublemakers in the classroom because their unconventional approaches to learning do not meet the teacher's expectations. Educators often find children who display creative tendencies to be difficult to manage. They consider them to be a threat to authority, undermining their role and status as the children do not conform to what are considered to be acceptable behaviours. Creative children may have the ability to challenge an educator's subject knowledge, skills and understanding in particular areas where their own abilities are of a high order. Creative children often work in unconventional ways implying a risk to the educator that things may 'get out of hand'. The time factor is also of concern for teachers. The pressures of the taught requirements of the National Curriculum may not allow for a process of exploration and investigation resulting in alternative ideas and solutions.

Educators need to accommodate the varying styles of learning that children display in order to assist them to meet their full potential. Above all we need to foster a climate of teaching and learning which inspires, stimulates, motivates and generates creative and imaginative thought, ideas and actions. *All Our Futures* (NACCCE, 1999: 36) cites Howard Gardner, 'each of us have a different mosaic of intelligences. Uniform schooling ignores these differences.'

TASK 1

Observe children in a variety of contexts, noting aspects of their responses that may indicate creative thought or action OR observe different teachers in varied curriculum areas and note the extent to which teaching styles encourage children's initiative and independent thinking.

Planning for creativity in teaching and learning

Three major themes emerge from study of early learning that are relevant to creativity in education but which also apply to thinking about the curriculum:

1 The need for continual sensory enrichment through 'concrete' or first-hand experience.
2 The search for personal meaning in order to interpret the world.
3 That *all* experience has the potential to form part of the internalised model of the world.

The tremendous burden of responsibility that educators of young children carry is that developmental continua begin at birth. Take art as an example, as Barnes (1987: 173) reminds us, 'for some children, their teacher may be the first person to draw children's attention to the appearance of things around them with any serious intention of initiating artistic learning'. With so much to do, educators of young children may feel that it is a question of priorities and they may need convincing that any serious attempt at art teaching is going to be worthwhile. This despite the fact young children naturally turn to drawing as a means to both respond to the world and recreate their thinking. Cox (1992: 5) shows how children develop their impressions of experience as a 'large repertoire of well-practised schemas' that they use to represent the world as they see it. Barnes (1987: 10) discusses the value of art in terms of visual literacy. 'Through a sharpened visual sense children learn to see much more and to see with greater insight than they otherwise would.'

Barnes also suggests that experience for children is often limited by being too generalised. The things that a child sees need to become personal and special to them. Thus the 'hooks of engagement' are important to recognise and develop. The task of the teacher is to introduce, organise and structure experience in ways that enable the child to focus upon it, to engage with the experience so that it meshes with their present thinking allowing it to become a potential part of their future way of conceptualising. Craft (2000) advocates the 'fostering of playful ideas', including supposing (which may involve pretending), 'imaging' and imagining (which she distinguishes from fantasising), arguing that these are all involved in play; the most significant of these qualities being imaginativeness. Barnes (1987: 10) talks about enabling children 'to discover the enjoyment of being able to see with the eye of an artist who is awake to the appearance of the surrounding world'. Such perception starts very early. It is this bond with the environment that we need to encourage if we are to promote visual literacy. 'Without developing visual literacy the relatively commonplace remains so', as Barnes (*ibid.*: 10) so eloquently puts it, going on to suggest that such awareness develops when we have the time to stop and look at things for ourselves.

Educators who make the time for really looking at things through any medium or subject that fosters engagement are more likely to develop children's 'literacies', visual and otherwise. Children make excellent and productive use of their time through play. The sensitive teacher will ensure that there is progression in the demands made upon the children's interpretation of experience. This would include the demand of being imaginative and the fostering of playful ideas. New ways of looking will be introduced, new techniques and a greater variety of 'media' with which to interpret experience will be provided and all the while the vocabulary of description, comparison and critical opinion will be developed. With this knowledge might the educator in the previous example of an art lesson, painting flowers, have responded differently to one child's individual and creative response and how might the lesson have been planned so that all the children were given access to, and credit for, this potential?

There are clear parallels here in other areas of creativity and readers should consider these when undertaking the tasks in the chapter. In terms of guidance as to how to foster sensory awareness, to allow engagement and to encourage playful approaches to interpretation, generally we become more aware of our environment when:

- it changes;
- we change in relation to it;
- we share it with others;
- there is a sudden contrast;
- we interact with it;
- it is closer to us or further away;
- we use one sense rather than another;
- it is presented to us in an unusual way;
- we are forced to concentrate hard on it or observe closely;
- we are called upon to create an environment rather than react to one.

Educators will readily see that the means for these 'exposures' lie within the creative arts, but not discretely so. While it is important that we recognise the unique contribution creative work can make to the child's understanding of the world, to treat it as a separate and unconnected way or knowing ignores its effect on other forms of learning. In fact, 'connectivity' is a feature of creativity. If we are to make essential links between our past, present and future experiences, then we need the opportunity to do this in our own terms. What is argued is that children need to be involved in creativity to *complete* their understanding so that they learn in a rounded and meaningful way. This theme is underlined by the inclusion of Art and Music in the National Curriculum and in the creative development aspect of the Physical Education curriculum, mainly through Dance and Gymnastics. Drama is included within English. The 'Areas of Learning' within the Curriculum Guidance for the Foundation Stage (QCA 2000) give more focus and scope within the experience offered and are exemplified in a succinct and direct manner.

While 'more formal' areas are generally accepted and well understood by educators, parents, and children, developing artistic and creative awareness is apparently less easy to understand and demonstrate. The process is important but the product may not be so easy to discern.

TASK 2

Reflect on the actual childhood experiences that are informing this remarkable piece of poetic writing by an eight-year-old girl. Then consider the vicarious experiences that have in all probability been gained through literature and the scope there would be for this within today's curriculum. What mental processes (e.g. connectivity), time, creative opportunities (especially the demand to be 'playful' and imaginative), and teaching approaches might have been encountered to enable this kind of response to experience?

Life Long or Horizon of Life
  My gaze travels down the cliff onto the shingle,
  Travels across the rocks
Onto the sand,
Into the sea.
Feathery breakers dancing, singing,
Below becalmed heavens.

And I think before me,
Into what, Life alone knows.

Into the dawn
When the sun shall bring back to life
The sleeping radience [sic] of the night.
A lonesome gull shatters my mind
Its mournful cry piercing the silence
But only vaguely.

I know of nothing but happiness,
The vast space behind me;
The prairie is my life,
The few trees and shrubs, happenings.
Rabbit warrens homes that my life has rested in,
And myself, centre of these thoughts,
Resting under an ever-lowering sun
The ever-deepening red and gold sky
In the heart of nature.
The buttercups waver around me.
A ghost of mist touches me with fingers
That dissolve into my hair.

I carelessly chew grass stalk

And sniff the cool air of the evening.
The gilded waves lap, subdued, against the shore.

No words shall ever describe
How I feel now
On this evening,
Where I sit.
And a secret wraps round my brain
That none shall ever know.

The secret of peace.

Creating a creative learning environment

Creativity emerges and grows in a learning environment which is rich in stimulus material designed to encourage a style of learning which promotes questioning, challenges convention, embraces problem solving and initiates independent thinking, expression and interpretation. We should never underestimate the impact that a vibrant, informative and strongly visual classroom makes on children's learning. The way the learning environment is perceived by children, as a support to the content of the teaching they receive, will, in turn, make a considerable difference to the level of pupil interest, motivation and engagement and ultimately to their attitude and approach to learning. The 'creative classroom' contributes to this process through the way it is arranged, the resources it provides, and the manner in which the visual and tactile material is communicated to the children to enrich their learning. Creativity is fostered by and through the senses and children therefore need an opportunity to explore avenues of learning which engage the full range of intelligences, involve them in 'hands-on' practical activity and stimulate thinking and problem solving from a variety of viewpoints. Children require access to the full curriculum, regardless of the subject barriers which we place around specific areas of learning and which often prohibit the cross-fertilisation of learning between one area of experience and another. Creativity transcends the 'ordinary and normal' and carries children to realms far beyond the minimum limits set by routine classroom tasks. The implication here is that, to engage with the creative impulse, children need a creative and stimulating environment.

While the potential to be creative and to think and act creatively is within all children, it does not happen in isolation. It is born out of interactions with the learning environment and sometimes collaboration with other learners although, as we have previously established, a characteristic of creativity is that children often prefer to work independently. A creative learning environment is one which allows for and positively encourages children to explore different approaches to learning, share and exchange ideas, consider alternative possibilities and engage in exploration, experimentation and investigation; a full and exciting voyage of discovery.

Creativity is an active process, and creative children will often appear restless until their curiosity has been satisfied. Commitment and conviction are key factors in creative teaching. This is not only found in austere learning environments but in those that are exciting, active, and participative and in tune with children's interests and experience. New areas of learning grow out of previous experience, knowledge and understanding.

Creativity is not an instant occurrence that happens in isolation but a process that requires a period of incubation. Children and educators therefore need to be given time in order to think and act creatively. The pressures of meeting the demands of the curriculum are not totally compatible with what the creative process requires. Duffy (1998: 26) states:

> Too often young children are given access to a narrow range of creative and imaginative experiences that are limited and superficial . . . these sorts of conditions lead to impoverished provision and depressed thinking. If children are to become competent . . . they need the opportunity and time to explore a wide range of experiences.

As educators we need regularly to review our practice with regard to the quality of learning experience offered to children and the richness of the environment in which we teach them. Children need opportunity to do the following:

- record from first-hand observation, experience and imagination, and explore ideas;
- ask and answer questions about the starting points for their work, and develop their ideas;
- investigate the possibilities of a range of materials and processes;
- try out tools and techniques and apply these to materials and processes;
- represent observations, ideas and feelings;
- review what they and others have done;
- identify what they might change or develop.

(QCA 1999: 4)

While the above statements are found in the art curriculum, the majority of them could appropriately apply in a general sense to learning across the whole curriculum. In essence, they are about the quality of opportunity and experience:

The environment in which we teach our children matters: it has to be home, resource centre, workshop and gallery all in one, because children are enabled or debilitated by being in it. It is a functional place and perhaps because of that it has failed for too long to attract the depth of thought and whole school policy making which it deserves.

(Morgan, in Jackson 1993: 10)

TASK 3

Undertake and analyse a learning activity designed to foster a creative response. Consider the role of questioning, children working collaboratively, modes of response and problem-solving opportunities OR track a child's experience across a typical school day, recording the range of learning opportunities and outcomes expected.

Possibilities and constraints within the curriculum

The National Curriculum emerged from a speech at Ruskin College, Oxford, in 1976, given by James Callaghan, the Prime Minister at the time. What became known as 'The Great Debate' led to a model of the curriculum which was fundamentally not new. Thus, the particular subjects and content to be studied were seen to be so deeply established as part of the social, economic and historical fabric of our society that it was difficult to change them. The 'Core' subjects or English, mathematics and science may be seen as dominating the curriculum in terms of time allocation and assessment requirements. Not least of the impacts this has had are that the Foundation Subjects, which traditionally had the greatest scope for cross-curricular work and creative approaches, have less time available to them.

The National Curriculum and the overload it produced for teachers, particularly in primary schools, led to early revisions for science and mathematics and a major revision for the whole curriculum in 1999 ready for the Millennium. The year 2000 also saw the advent of the Curriculum Guidance for the Foundation Stage, encompassing pre-school and the reception class and schemes of work produced by the Qualifications and Curriculum Authority for the Foundation Subjects. It is arguable now whether the National Curriculum fulfils the original aims of being broad, balanced, relevant and accessible.

As the most easily demonstrable and measurable characteristics of the curriculum have been given preference, pupils have become increasingly disaffected, teacher autonomy and initiative have been systematically eroded and it is more than likely that enthusiasm and initiative, the very stuff of creativity, has been ground down too. This developing schism in curriculum provision has been a long-term concern since the inception of the National Curriculum.

What scope is there then for interpretation and innovation by educators wishing to take a creative stance to learning and teaching? Clearly, proactive, rather than reactive educators, who are driven by their own standards and belief in what is essential and valuable for their pupils will always be able to 're-engineer' the curriculum. Such educators are not alone. There is a powerful lobby for Arts Education, and in 1999 this found its voice through the National Advisory Committee on Creative and Cultural Education. The NACCCE report *All Our Futures* addressed the economic, technological, social and personal purposes of the curriculum and empowered all those advocating creativity in the curriculum. The summary document suggests:

> Creative teaching means teaching creatively, and, more pertinent here, teaching for creativity. Teaching creatively involves teachers using imaginative approaches to make learning more interesting, exciting and effective. Teaching for creativity means teachers developing young people's own creative thinking or behaviour, and includes teaching creatively. This comprises encouraging young people to believe in their creative potential and giving them the confidence to try; identifying their creative abilities and helping them to find their creative strengths; and fostering their creativity by developing ordinary abilities and skills, and common capacities and sensitivities, and understanding what is involved in being creative.
>
> (NACCCE 2000: 6)

We believe there is considerable mileage in drawing out some key characteristics of creative learning from the Report and applying these to the curriculum. Further, the Report acknowledges that, in the current climate, 'value' rests upon assessment, and insights are given into the ways in which we can both recognise and assess creativity. Four features of creativity are outlined which can be used in considering any aspect of the curriculum both for planning and assessment purposes.

1 Using imagination
   (a) Imaginative activity is the process of generating something original, providing an alternative to the expected, the conventional or the routine. This means planning in an open-ended way and expecting that children will not conform. The 'tyranny of the right answer', where children continually aspire to guess what the teacher wants by way of a 'correct' response, is the most serious impediment to both thinking and creativity. This has major implications for planning in a way that is not too tight or prescriptive and will immediately be seen

as problematic for those teachers for whom this is antipathetic to their usual practice.

(b) Imagination is often most vividly seen when thought is embodied in movement. This we equate to 'performance'. While we may recognise it in the 'gross' motor movements of dance or gymnastics, as teachers we may not be attuned to noticing it in the subtleties of 'fine' movements that may be indicative of creativity; such as the deftness of the use of line in drawing, the sweep of a brush in painting or the expressiveness of a gesture in dance, drama or speech.

(c) Imaginative activity as an outward manifestation of mental play may indicate that there is serious intention directed towards a creative purpose. The child may well be seeking to express, externalise and realise thought which otherwise cannot find expression in a tangible way, for example, through talk. Thus creativity is seen to be generative.

2 Pursuing purposes

'Applied' imagination may manifest itself in the need to take an idea further indicated by enquiry, engagement and or practical investigation. This may be seen as exploring the possibilities of an idea or testing a creative hypothesis. Common examples are found in play where the direction of the activity is indicative of the mental processes and connections that underpin it.

3 Being original

Notwithstanding that agreement about what this actually means is problematic, there is general understanding that originality can be:

(a) Individual – a person's work may be original relative to his or her own previous work and output (ipsative assessment). Characteristics may be that the new work takes an element of the previous work further or stands in contrast to it but where the previous work has provided the starting point.

(b) Relative – a child's work may be original in relation to that of others (peers) involved, by standing out from the norm or the conventions of the group.

(c) Historic – the work may be original in terms of anyone's previous output and so be uniquely original.

4 Judging value

(a) Value judgements made through evaluating the task in hand, for example, notions of the decisions made or progress towards outcomes being effective, useful, enjoyable, satisfying, valid, tenable, etc., according to the activity in question.

(b) Signs of playing with ideas and trying out possibilities may indicate creative activity. The sequence of attempts, errors made, dead-ends reached, backtracking, choices made, avenues pursued, solutions accepted or rejected all indicate a process at work.

(c) Shifts in focus or attention may indicate a reflective stance. Helping children to manage the interaction between generative and evaluative thinking is a crucial aspect of creative growth.

Experienced educators will readily identify that the unpredictable nature of many of these characteristics, the lack of control over direction and variables and the behaviours that children are likely to exhibit in the course of creative activity are exactly those that we seek to 'plan out' of the curriculum. Young children are generally quite uninhibited about exploring their world by using their creative senses but conventions, social norms and continued attention to preferred modes of learning or responses discourage the use of some senses and skills and we come to rely on those that we use most often. In Piagetian terms as we develop cognitively we move from the concrete to the abstract. However, this is not a passive process, it is rather the most demanding call on both the learner's and the educator's personal energies and resources. 'In time one visits and revisits the same general principles, rendering them increasingly more abstract and formal, more precise, more powerful, more generative' (Bruner 1971: 122).

The mechanism for this is summarised by the Bullock Report appropriately entitled *A Language for Life*:

> It is a confusion of everyday thought that we tend to regard 'knowledge' as something that exists independently of someone who knows. 'What is known' must in fact be brought to life afresh within every 'knower' by his own efforts.
>
> (DES 1975: 50)

TASK 4

Revisit the poetic writing 'Horizon of Life' and, using the four areas drawn from the NACCCE (1999) Report listed above, see if you are able to pass a more objective assessment on the work than you could previously have done. What indicates originality, creative thought or action? Is creativity assessable in other modes of activity using this model?

Summary and key points

Many adults in later life find the need to re-educate the senses, dulled by years of abstinence or the 'ellipses' that modern life imposes. Part of the educator's task in developing the whole child is to make creative and sensual experience sufficiently worthwhile that the child willingly continues to engage in the broadest spectrum of experiences. One aim of developing creativity must be to stimulate awareness of self, others and the world. This is in itself knowledge. However, no knowledge exists in any meaningful form unless it finds expression through which the consciousness is exposed. 'A long-term aim of visual literacy is to make children so aware of their surroundings that they go on looking when they grow up so increasingly applying stored experiences to new situations' (Barnes 1987: 13). This ought to be generalised as a principle underlying all literacies. Just as art might be seen as a continuum of awareness, all learning should be viewed in this continuous and progressive manner. This might encourage a deeper consideration of the nature, purpose and value of the curriculum than we are presently given scope for in our adherence to the prescriptive frameworks that have been imposed upon us.

Theoretical perspectives and the premise of a broad, balanced and relevant curriculum continue to validate educators' professionalism and autonomy in making decisions about what, when and how to teach children. The attitudes and behaviours invoked through creative activity are essential to children's success, self-image and positive contribution to the future:

> We might ask, as a criterion for any subject taught in Primary school, whether, when fully developed, it is worth an adult's knowing, and whether having known it as a child makes us a better adult. If the answer to both questions is negative or ambiguous, then the material is cluttering up the curriculum.
>
> (Bruner 1963: 52)

A further way of looking at this is to ask what sort of enjoyable and natural ways of exploring and responding to the world do adults discourage in children and are there compelling reasons for doing so?

Questions to aid reflection

1 Consider how your education prepared you for life as you experience it now. What elements of the curriculum contributed most to the abilities, skills or attributes you most value and use, or would aspire to, if you had the chance?

2 Imagination can be described as 'internalised play'. What life experiences and play activities do children need if they are to have the kinds of imagination that might be required in the future?

3 Think of examples of children's responses or actions that we treasure precisely because they failed (just) to get things 'right'. When and why do you think adults and educators stop accepting and rewarding attempt over precision?

Acknowledgement

Kelling County Primary School for permission to use 'Life Long or Horizon of Life' from *Colours of Hope*, an anthology of children's work

Annotated bibliography

Barnes, R. (1987) *Teaching Art to Young Children 4-9*, London: Allen & Unwin.
 This text is much more than an art book: it provides a passionate rationale for the Arts.
Craft, A. (2000) *Creativity Across the Primary Curriculum*, London: Routledge.
 The full range of the curriculum is considered while identifying the role of creativity in teaching and learning.
Duffy, B. (1998) *Supporting Creativity and Imagination in the Early Years*, Buckingham: Open University Press.
 A comprehensive consideration of creativity in early learning, providing a sound theoretical viewpoint illuminating aspects of good practice.

Bibliography

Barnes, R. (1987) *Teaching Art to Young Children 4–9*. London: Allen & Unwin.
Best, D. (1983) 'Can creativity be taught?', *Journal of the Institute of Art Education* 7(1) Brunet, J.S. (1963) *The Process of Education*. New York: Vintage Books.
Bruner, J.S. (1971) *The Relevance of Education*, London: Allen & Unwin.
Calouste Gulbenkian Foundation (1982) *The Arts in Schools*, London: Calouste Gulbenkian Foundation.
Cox, M. (1992) *Children's Drawings*, Harmondsworth: Penguin.
Craft, A. (2000) *Creativity Across the Primary Curriculum*, London: Routledge.
DES (1975) *A Language for Life*, London: HMSO.
Duffy, B. (1998) *Supporting Creativity and Imagination in the Early Years*, Buckingham: Open University Press.
Gardner, H. (1984) *Frames of Mind: The Theory of Multiple Intelligencies*, London: Heinemann.
Jacobson, S. (1983) *Meta-cognition: Prescriptions for Some Ailing Educational Processes*, Cupertimo, CA: Meta Publications.
Lowenfeld, V. and Brittain, W.L. (1975) *Creative and Mental Growth*, New York: Macmillan.

Morgan. M. in Jackson, M. (1993) *Creative Display and Environment,* London: Hodder and Stoughton.

National Advisory Committee on Creative and Cultural Education (NACCCE) (1999) *All Our Futures: Creativity, Culture and Education*, Sudbury: DfEE.

National Advisory Committee on Creative and Cultural Education (NACCCE) (2000) *All Our Futures: A Summary,* National Campaign for the Arts.

QCA (1999) *Art and Design: The National Curriculum for England*, London: DfEE.

QCA (2000) *Curriculum Guidance for the Foundation Stage*, London: DfEE.

Ross, M. (1978) *The Creative Arts*, London: Heinemann.

Educating All: Towards Inclusive Classroom Practice for Children with Special Educational Needs

8

Carrie Weston

Introduction

What does inclusion mean? That's easy! It means 'incorporation, assimilation, comprehension, admission, integration' (Roget's *Thesaurus of English Words and Phrases*). Yet, in education, 'inclusion' seems somehow to lack a universally shared meaning. What *does* inclusion mean for those working in the classroom?

The placement of a child within a mainstream school cannot be a measure of inclusion; it is what goes on within the school, classroom and community that creates 'inclusive practice' – or not. In addition, the notion of 'inclusion', particularly for those pupils described as having 'special educational needs', sits awkwardly alongside some other educational policies, such as league tables, national standards, selection and setting. The pressure to raise standards of attainment has often meant that children with special educational needs have been peripheral to the core concerns of schools. Still, the language of inclusion is now widely used by government, local education authorities (LEAs) and schools in policies, guidelines and legislation. So what does it mean for those working in classrooms and, particularly, for those children who are described as having 'special educational needs'?

By the end of this chapter you should have:

- gained an understanding of the historical context and development of inclusive education for children with special educational needs;
- been introduced to the requirements relating to inclusion laid down in the National Curriculum and standards for gaining qualified teacher status (QTS);

- identified your own perspectives and development needs relating to inclusion.

Inclusion has been described as a process, a journey rather than a destination (Mittler 2000). This is, perhaps, because classrooms, curricula and school systems evolve over time and are shaped by various agendas, policies, legislation and ideologies. This process is a continuous one, as educators strive to understand the influences of the learning environment, teaching content and approaches on pupils and reflect upon ways of improving what they do.

The National Curriculum, Ofsted and Standards for Qualified Teacher Status (QTS) now require those who work in classrooms to reflect on and promote inclusion in their practice. As well as an understanding of what is *required* of classroom practitioners, it is necessary to understand the processes that have brought us to conclude that inclusion is both *right* and *necessary*. In other words, understanding what has gone on in the past can illuminate the present and provide a guide to where we are going in the future.

Inclusion and special educational needs

The term 'special educational needs' (SEN) is arguably an outdated one. It will be used in this chapter in the absence of any readily available and universally accepted alternative. Although the term *additional needs* is emerging in some literature and policies, at the current time 'special educational needs' is a more widely applied term. However, it can be an emotive term and one that carries many meanings for many people in many different situations.

Task 1

Do you have any experience of 'special educational needs'?
This may be a memory from your own school days, current experience in the classroom or personal experience.

Categorise your experiences/thoughts/images relating to special educational needs into:

positive   negative

If you are able to, discuss and compare with a friend or colleague.

This task is one I have often asked groups of student teachers, practising educators, classroom assistants and parents to participate in. Frequently, most experiences are classified as negative and 'special educational needs' is associated with descriptions such as 'struggling', 'being pitied', 'needing help' or 'being different'. The perception, whether it comes from personal, childhood or practitioner experience, is often one of *difference* or *difficulty*. Yet, one in five of children in classrooms throughout the UK are described as having some kind of special educational need. When we stop to think of the many meanings we attach to the term SEN, and how few of these are positive, then it is possible to understand the view taken by Jonathan Solity (1991) that 'special needs' is itself a discriminatory concept. If this is true, then 20 per cent of our children are experiencing such discrimination on a daily basis.

The notion of special educational need is complex. Who has needs, and who doesn't? Who decides these things anyway? We all have our weaknesses and we all have our strengths; we all have our goals and our limitations. My thoughts turn to tennis here. Having taken lessons for many years, I still find myself unable to play a decent game of tennis. I have made little progress in my learning of the skills of tennis, despite my best efforts. Nevertheless, I thoroughly enjoy knocking the ball over (or, more often, into) the net with anyone willing to join in with me. I can even feel a fairly competent player under such circumstances. I experience much less enjoyment, and far less self-esteem, when I can see my lack of skill irritating my opponent. I feel absolutely miserable about playing tennis when success is valued in terms of winning games rather than, say, improving the number of volleys returned. Under these circumstances my strongest inclination is to give up altogether. My low level of skill in tennis is certainly not an important classroom issue, yet it demonstrates some of the complexities attached to 'need'. It is the *situation* that often defines the need; it is the *context* that can create the barriers; it is the nature of the *task* that can define success or failure.

Task 2

Can you think of any experiences that have shaped your understanding of the notion of 'need'?

Think of a skill or a task that you feel confident performing (situation 1).

Think of a skill or a task that you feel less confident about (situation 2).

Now fill in the grid in Figure 8.1.

Describe your enthusiasm for/enjoyment of the task in:
Situation 1
Situation 2

Describe your feelings about yourself doing this task (self-esteem)
Situation 1
Situation 2

Where does your motivation come from?
Situation 1
Situation 2

Figure 8.1   Confidence levels

In order to investigate the many meanings conjured up by the term 'special educational needs', it is necessary to understand something of the origins and development of 'schooling for all' in the UK and, in turn, consider what this has meant for children with 'special educational needs'.

Pre-1870

Before 1870, the education a child received was determined largely by class. For working-class children, a basic education may have been obtained through Sunday School (funded and run by churches and attended by the majority of poor children), a factory school (set up by a philanthropic organisation to teach basic skills to poor children of factory workers) or a dame school (a 'one-woman' affair set up in the teacher's home where children could receive lessons for a small fee). There were also 'ragged schools' which provided a basic, free education to children considered too poor or too dirty to be accepted elsewhere. Education for the working classes was *ad hoc*, the quality of teaching was not regulated or monitored and schooling was not compulsory. For many children, getting any kind of education depended both on what was available locally and the financial means of their parents. For most, the education available finished at primary level.

For middle-class children, education usually took place at home either with a parent or governess. When they were older, boys might be sent away to private schools, while girls continued to learn at home or at small private schools.

The 1870 Education Act

From 1870 a state system of education began to develop. The Education Act of 1870 established elementary schooling, although this was not free. With a weekly fee of up to nine pence per child, many children were still unable to benefit from the developing education system. School attendance became compulsory in 1880, but it was not universally free until 1891 and opportunities to enter secondary education without paying did not begin to develop until after the 1902 Education Act.

We need to consider for a moment what led to the development of the beginning of the state system of education. Rather than purely a move towards social justice, the development of universal free education came about as a means of social organisation and national needs. The 1867 Franchise Act saw the right to vote extended to working-class men for the first time. This extension of enfranchisement gave rise to the need for a more educated population. In an increasingly industrialised nation, a need for a more skilled workforce was perceived by the 'ruling' classes; a growing population needed to understand basic skills in order to be able to work, raise a family and live within the law.

Although there was no National Curriculum in existence, the basic timetable was almost universal as it consisted of 'the 3 Rs' (reading, writing and arithmetic), plus religious exercises. Emphasis was placed on the neatness of handwriting, and the government gave small grants for the teaching of skills it considered 'necessary'. For working-class girls, this included cookery, laundry work, needlework and domestic duties in preparation for their lives ahead as mothers or in domestic service. Universal free education, then, can be seen as originating not to develop and educate the individual, but as a means of schooling the 'masses ' in the skills needed by, and perceived desirable by, society. The needs of, and concerns for, individual learners were not a part of this framework.

The Victorian classroom was a strict, formal setting. Children who found learning difficult could be harshly treated, with corporal punishment being the norm. Even being left-handed was strongly discouraged. Behaviour that did not conform to expected standards, for whatever reasons, was not tolerated.

Intelligence testing

In 1904 the French government commissioned Simon and Binet to devise a test to identify children with 'inferior intelligence'. These were children who, it was considered, would not benefit from ordinary schooling. The Simon–Binet test (1905) was the first published intelligence test. This saw a rapid rise in the development of intelligence quotient (IQ) testing, particularly in the United States where the Simon–Binet test later became the Stanford–Binet test after development at Stanford University. The development of IQ tests led to the belief that people had *fixed* and determinable levels of intelligence. However, these early tests were often flawed by their bias towards those who devised them – namely white, middle-class men. It should be noted that before 1937, the collected mean scores of women on the Stanford–Binet test were 10 points lower than the male score! Intelligence testing led to the belief that some children, those with low 'IQ' scores, were 'uneducable'.

The 1944 Education Act

Although since the 1890s local authorities had been expected to make provision for blind and deaf children, and some authorities provided care for children considered to be 'mentally defective', this was not necessarily educational provision. Many children, across the whole spectrum of 'need', were not acknowledged within the state education system.

The end of the Second World War saw great changes in British society which were reflected in the education system. Legislation in 1944 raised the school-leaving age to 15, providing mass secondary education, in addition to primary education. For the first time, local authorities were called upon to provide 'for pupils who suffer from any disability of mind or body' and to provide free medical treatment, milk and meals for pupils. In the consultation preceding the 1944 Education Act it was estimated that 14–17 per cent of all children were 'disabled' to some degree, and that these children should, on the whole, benefit from mainstream state schooling. Yet, despite this, the post-war years saw the most dramatic rise in the number of 'special schools' established. That is not to suggest that the 1944 Act actively promoted segregation, the establishment of separate provision for children with special educational needs was never, in fact, state policy. However, in a nation impoverished by war, where class sizes were large and many educators were ill trained, the early notion of 'inclusion' evident in the 1944 Act was never followed through or practicable. In addition, the Act introduced categories of handicap that clearly located educational 'problems' within the child, rather than the education and opportunities offered to him or her. This gave rise to 'specialist' provision for children with 'problems'. Such children, it was perceived, needed something beyond the remit of the ordinary educator in the ordinary classroom.

The categories of handicap identified by the 1944 Act were: defective of speech; blind; partially sighted; deaf; partially deaf; delicate; diabetic; educationally subnormal; maladjusted; physically handicapped. This was very much a *medical model*, whereby children could be 'diagnosed' and then allocated to a category. Intelligence testing (also used to allocate 'brighter' pupils to grammar schools) was used to place children with a measured IQ of less than 50 out of the education system entirely and in the care of health authorities, effectively denying them any educational opportunity at all. Rather than inclusion, then, it can be argued that the 1944 Education Act supported *exclusion* based on the idea of 'measurable' pupil difference.

During the 1950s and 1960s Britain saw greater economic prosperity which led to greater funding of the educational system. Also during this period more women than ever before entered the employment market and there was a rise in the number of migrants, particularly from the Caribbean, South Asia and Ireland, generally taking up lower paid manual work as more and more people moved into service sector employment. Grammar schools existed alongside the new 'secondary modern', yet plenty of evidence suggests that the divide was less one of 'ability' and more one of wealth, class and opportunity. However, the grammar school system continued to prevail (and, indeed, in some areas still exists today) and more special schools were established. Therefore, the concept that children should be separated and educated according to ability or *dis*ability was an accepted one.

The 1967 Plowden Report

The Plowden Report, *Children and their Primary Schools* (1967), looked at educational experiences and attainment from nursery to the end of the primary phase. It was the first report on schools that acknowledged a relationship between poverty and educational attainment. The Plowden Report recommended that resources should be channelled to compensate for disadvantage, such as the expansion of nursery provision in the poorest areas.

The 1970 Education Act (Handicapped Children)

This act placed responsibility for the education of children with special educational needs with local education authorities rather than health authorities. For the first time, all children became entitled to an education. As a result of this Act, special schools were categorised as catering for: moderate learning difficulties (MLD), severe learning difficulties (SLD) or severe subnormal difficulties (SSD).

Task 3

Read these extracts from *Children with Special Needs in the Infants' School* by Lesley Webb, published in 1967.

Most teachers have to deal occasionally, and some often, with difficult children. Whether these children are described as maladjusted, delinquent, backward, underprivileged or simply as naughty they present teachers with problems of discipline, learning and social training which often seem (and sometimes are) insoluble in the everyday classroom situation . . .

A teacher is a specialist in her own right. Her special skill is the promotion of learning; and she cannot help a child if he is locked in his own unhappiness, handicapped by dullness, or so socially underprivileged that communication does not exist between them . . .

Unlike a sociologist, a teacher does not have to look for her sample. It comes to her. Every child of five who is not grossly physically or mentally defective, or of that tiny minority that receives independent education, comes into an ordinary Infants' school. Despite lazy, inadequate, seclusive or migrant parents who may have evaded all the pre-school services for their children, the legal necessity for school attendance brings them to official notice at last.

How many 'labels' can you find in these extracts? What do you think these mean, and how do you feel about them?

What responsibilities do schools and teachers seem to have in identifying and teaching children with special educational needs?

Where does the blame for 'problems' seem to rest?

The 1978 Warnock Report

The Labour government commissioned Mary Warnock to investigate and make recommendations in the education of handicapped children and young people. The final report was delivered to a new Conservative government in 1978 and informed the 1981 Education Act. The Warnock Report was a milestone in the education of children with special educational needs as, for the first time, it was recognised that needs could be *'fluctuating and contextually defined'* (DES 1978). In other words, 'needs' were not fixed within children and were not 'deficits' in need of remediation. A 'continuum' of need was recognised, along with the fact that needs could be short term or long term. In addition, the report also recognised that *context* could create need; schools themselves were sometimes responsible for the difficulties experienced by children. The Warnock Report outlined the necessity for schools to be able to recognise and respond to need through differentiating the curriculum, thus enabling more children with special educational needs to attend a mainstream school. Importantly, the report also stressed the need for schools to work in partnership with parents in order to achieve the best for children with special educational needs. Although the word 'inclusion' was not a part of the Warnock Report, it did argue for the *integration* of pupils with special educational needs. Integration, in this sense, implies that children with special educational needs can be accommodated, or made to fit, within mainstream schooling.

In her report, Mary Warnock identified that one in five of all pupils had some kind of special educational need at some time during their school life. This figure of 20 per cent represented a wide spectrum of pupils and needs, dispelling the myth of a hard and fast divide between children with 'handicap' and those without. Of this 20 per cent figure, Warnock recognised 2 per cent experienced 'severe' need which required some kind of exceptional provision.

The 1981 Education Act

This Act embodied the principle of integrating children with special educational needs into mainstream schooling. This was achieved by placing responsibility for the provision of education for children with special educational needs with local authorities and deeming that, wherever practicable, this should occur within a mainstream school. Local education authorities became responsible for the identification and assessment of special educational needs, which could be carried out through a multidisciplinary team (educational psychologists, medical professionals, social services, speech and language therapists, occupational therapists and other professionals) and possibly result in the issuing of a *statement of special educational needs* where appropriate. It was envisaged that the 2 per cent of pupils identified by Warnock as having severe special educational needs would be those assessed and, where necessary, issued with statements.

A statement might recommend a placement for a child within a special school or within a mainstream school with additional and appropriate support and resources. The 1981 Act removed the previous categories of handicap, and placed emphasis on the individual needs of the child. Where a statement was issued, it would identify these individual needs.

The 1981 Act provided, for the first time, a definition of 'special educational needs'. Children have a learning difficulty if:

> they have significantly greater difficulty in learning than the majority of children of their age, or they have a disability which prevents or hinders them from making use of the educational facilities generally provided for children of their age (DFE 1993).

The 1981 Education Act also enshrined the concept of partnership with parents. The rights of parents had already been established in the 1980 Education Act, which provided parents with choice in selecting a school for their child.

The 1988 Education Reform Act (ERA)

This Act established the principle that all children have an entitlement to access a 'broad and balanced' curriculum, to be followed in all state schools by pupils between the ages of 5 and 16. National tests (SATs) were introduced to measure the performance of both pupils and schools. While this seems to promote inclusion through universal entitlement, other elements of the Act seemed to discourage inclusion. The publication of 'league tables' was intended to indicate the success, or otherwise, of schools. Parents could see how many children within each school reached nationally prescribed 'standards', through testing, at the end of each Key Stage. In addition, schools were given greater control over their budget, allowing head teachers and governing bodies to make decisions about resourcing within their schools. The effects of this, when combined with the emergence of parental choice, were to create a 'market place' where children with special educational needs quickly became the least valuable currency. A high number of pupils with special educational needs in a school would not benefit its 'league position'; schools lower down in league tables would not attract the mobile (and, generally, middle-class) parents seeking the 'best' school for their child, thus creating 'successful' and 'unsuccessful' schools by a process of furtive selection conveniently called 'choice'. The process of national testing of pupils led to a narrowing of what was regarded as 'success' and, at the same time, created many 'unsuccessful' pupils. While an emphasis on attainment in schools is most desirable, it requires a deeper understanding of what 'attainment' is than simply pre-set national standards against which all pupils are measured. In many ways, despite its rhetoric of 'access for all', the 1988 Education Reform

Act was a major step backwards for pupils with special educational needs, as their concerns were more removed from the central aims of schools than ever before. The immediate response to the 'problem' of children with special educational needs was to modify the National Curriculum for some children or 'disapply' others altogether. This just brings into question the claim of universal statutory entitlement.

The National Curriculum for all pupils still exists, and with it the potential of entitlement and access for all pupils. Changes to the original National Curriculum have been made over recent years. In 1999, the re-written *National Curriculum Handbook* (DfEE 1999) included for the first time an overarching statement on inclusion which makes clear, 'the principles schools must follow in their teaching right across the curriculum, to ensure that all pupils have the chance to succeed, whatever their individual needs and the potential barriers to their learning may be' (*ibid.*: 3). This concept goes much further than the Warnock notion of *integration* enshrined in the 1981 Education Act. *Inclusion* implies fundamental changes to schools and teaching to establish equal access from the outset.

The National Curriculum now requires all educators to do the following:

- set suitable learning challenges;
- respond to pupils' diverse learning needs;
- overcome potential barriers to learning and assessment for individuals and groups of pupils.

Educators are required to be able to do the following:

- differentiate the curriculum offered;
- choose appropriate knowledge, skills and understanding to meet individual needs (from earlier or later stages of the National Curriculum where necessary);
- plan with knowledge of legislation and requirements on equal opportunities, covering race, gender and disability;
- take specific action to respond to pupils' diverse needs;
- plan for full participation;
- plan for pupils who are learning English as an additional language.

The means to achieve this will be located in the values, practices and support offered by LEAs and schools, and in training for teachers and others working in schools.

The 1994 Code of Practice

Although this was not legislation, schools and Local Education Authorities (LEAs) were bound by law to take account of the Code of Practice on Special Educational Needs. This document was designed to regulate and guide practices in schools relating to identification, assessment and provision for children with special educational needs, and, in a revised form (DfES 2001a), guides these practices today.

The Code of Practice requires all schools to have a member (or members) of staff responsible for the coordination of provision for pupils with special educational needs. This meant that the role of SENCO (Special Educational Needs Coordinator) was created in all schools. In addition, all schools were required to produce a special educational needs policy which must be made available to parents. As part of an Ofsted inspection, the special educational needs policy and practices is looked at in all schools in relation to the Code of Practice (DfES 2001b).

In order to establish some form of uniformity in how schools identify, assess and provide for children with special educational needs, the 1994 Code of Practice established a 'five-stage model' intended to represent the spectrum of special educational needs in schools, see Figure 8.2.

Stage 1
Initial concern about a pupil recorded. Monitoring and provision by class teacher. Individual Education Plan (IEP) optional.
Stage 2
SENCO involved in consultation and planning for pupil. Appropriate targets for pupil set and monitored. IEP required with regular review.
Stage 3
Outside agencies involved in assessment and planning for pupil in collaboration with teacher, SENCO and parents. IEP and regular review required.
Stage 4
Formal assessment of pupil carried out by local education authority to inform decision on issuing of statement.
Stage 5
Statement issued by local education authority. In most cases, the pupil will attend a mainstream school with recommended support or provision. In a few cases a special school placement recommended. Annual review of statement required.

Figure 8.2 The 1994 Code of Practice five-stage model

Individual Education Plans (IEPs)

IEPs are records of the strategies employed to enable a child to progress. They should record short-term targets for the child, teaching strategies to be used, provision required and success criteria. IEPs should also include a stated review date, consultation with parents and child and must record outcomes at the time of review.

The Code of Practice 2001

There has been considerable evaluation of the 1994 Code of Practice, resulting in the revised Code issued in 2001. The main criticism of the original Code of Practice was its bureaucratic nature and the immense amount of paperwork involved. In addition, if you look again at Figure 8.2, you will see that beyond Stage 1, a child with special educational needs seems to be implicitly outside the knowledge and professionalism of the class teacher. This seems to suggest that there are 'ordinary' teachers who teach 'ordinary' pupils and there are children with special educational needs who require specialist intervention. Another difficulty with the five-stage model is that it tends to look like a 'ladder'. The further 'up' the stages a child gets, then the greater the support available becomes. The danger inherent in this model is that it encourages momentum towards the higher stages in order to access more support and, potentially, funding. One outcome has certainly been that more pupils have been issued with statements of special educational need than was intended. The original figure of 2 per cent has risen to over 3 per cent. The first issue of the Code of Practice could be described as still largely a deficit model. This sees the cause of special educational needs as being within the child and in need of remediation. Such a view does little to enhance the skills of class teachers and support staff in making classrooms inclusive. 'Support' in many cases is not embedded in the practices of ordinary, everyday classrooms. In some cases, children with special educational needs are grouped together within the classroom; in other cases they are withdrawn from the classroom for lessons or part of the school day. The nature of 'support' in this context is often a learning support assistant (LSA), sometimes also known as support assistants (SAs), Special Support Assistants (SSAs) or Teaching Assistants (TAs). This creates the paradox that the children with the most need are supported by the adults with the least qualifications and pay. This is not to suggest that support staff are not highly valuable within the classroom (most are worth their weight in gold), but it does raise questions about the nature of the equality of opportunity offered to children with special educational needs.

Following wide consultation, in January 2002, a revised Code of Practice on Special Educational Needs came into force. As well as reducing the paperwork involved, the five-stage model was replaced with a two-tier system, although still retaining statutory assessment and statementing, see Figure 8.3. Formal assessment and statementing only takes place beyond the level of 'School Action Plus'.

School Action	A whole-school approach to SEN, SENCO to work with teachers to plan collaboratively for a range of pupils. Training and support to widen skills within schools. Move from individual, specialised support towards a widening of available resources and knowledge.
School Action Plus	Outside agency support in conjunction with school. Coordinated by SENCO. Support offered may be for training and development of teachers/support staff within the school.

Figure 8.3   2002 Code of Practice two-tier system

The main features of the revised Code of Practice are:

- re-establishment of the right of all children to a mainstream education (supported by the Special Educational Needs and Disability Discrimination Act, 2001, see below);
- the setting of high expectations and suitable standards for all children;
- strengthening of the rights of parents *and* children in decision-making, working in partnership, participation, appeal procedures and access to information;
- a 'graduated response', which requires schools and early years settings to monitor *all* children and reflect the continuum of special educational needs in their provision;
- an expectation that each school will provide appropriate time, resources and training for the SENCO to carry out the role of special needs coordination effectively;
- greater emphasis on the benefits of schools working in collaboration with outside agencies such as health services, educational psychology, behaviour support, social services and others.

The revised Code of Practice on Special Educational Needs leans far more towards inclusive practices than its predecessor. The emphasis is on the widening of the range of skills and resources regularly available within schools in order to reflect a greater range of pupil abilities. There is less emphasis upon individual, specialised support.

> The way in which a school meets the needs of *all* children has a direct bearing on the nature of the additional help required by children with special educational needs, and on the point at which additional help is required. The key to meeting the needs of all children lies in the teacher's knowledge of each child's skills and abilities and the teacher's ability to match this knowledge to finding ways of providing appropriate access to the curriculum for every child.
>
> (30, para 5:37)

Individual Education Plans (IEPs) are still an important part of the Code of Practice, but there is more emphasis on the involvement of parents and children, and the collaboration between class teachers and others involved in the education and well-being of the child.

The revised Code is supported by the Special Needs and Disability Discrimination Act 2001 requiring, by law, that schools and LEAs do not treat disabled pupils less favourably than other pupils. Adjustments must be made (at both curriculum and physical environment level) so that pupils with special needs and disabilities are not placed at a disadvantage. In addition, the document *Inclusive Schooling* (DfES 2001) provides schools and LEAs with guidelines on developing effective inclusion, safeguarding the interests of all pupils, ensuring that inclusion remains compatible with the efficient education of all children and cites instances where it may not always be possible to include specific children in mainstream schools within the current statutory framework. *Intervening Early* (DfES 2002) is a report that provides a 'snapshot' of current good practice and approaches in primary schools that help children to get the best from school. The *Index for Inclusion* (CSIE 2000) is designed to support schools with the process of developing inclusion in schools.

Standards for the award of Qualified Teacher Status (QTS)

The Teacher Training Agency (TTA) has set standards for the award of QTS (DfES/TTA 2002). These standards relate to the following:

- Professional Values and Practice:
- Knowledge and Understanding;
- Teaching.

In order to gain QTS, training teachers must know, understand and be able to perform the requirements laid down in specific outcome statements. Many of these relate to inclusive practice within the classroom. Those awarded

QTS must understand and uphold the professional code of the General Teaching Council for England. The following list indicates the numbers of the standards relating to inclusive practices. Those listed under Professional Values and Practice are outlined here to provide a flavour of the requirements.

Professional Values and Practice

1.1 They have high expectations of all pupils; respect their social, cultural linguistic, religious and ethnic backgrounds; and are committed to raising their educational achievement.

1.2 They treat pupils consistently, with respect and consideration, and are concerned for their development as learners.

1.3 They demonstrate and promote the positive values, attitudes and behaviour that they expect from their pupils.

1.4 They can communicate sensitively and effectively with parents and carers, recognising their roles in pupils' learning, and their rights, responsibilities and interests in this.

There are also requirements for: Knowledge and Understanding (2.4, 2.6), Planning, Expectations and Targets (3.1.1, 3.1.2), Monitoring and Assessment (3.2.4, 3.2.6, 3.2.7) and Teaching and Class Management (3.3.1, 3.3.4, 3.3.8, 3.3.9, 3.3.13, 3.3.14). In meeting these standards, it is acceptable for those training to have the help and guidance of an experienced teacher. This recognises the benefits of an apprenticeship model and the value of colleagues working together to develop effective practices. There is clearly no reason why this model of working should apply only to those currently in training or in their induction year.

Developing skills and confidence

In the report *Special Educational Needs: A Mainstream Issue*, the Audit Commission (2002) recommended that schools audit the training needs of all staff (including non-teaching staff) in relation to SEN and respond accordingly. LEAs are encouraged to develop training programmes for their schools and extend the role of special schools within the authority. Special schools should provide both on-site training for mainstream colleagues as well as developing two-way learning opportunities between special and mainstream schools.

Task 4

What training/professional development opportunities exist within your local LEA?

Are there any special units or special schools within the area?

Would any local schools be willing to let you make informal visits to observe practice, or shadow the SENCO for a day?

Be prepared for schools to say 'no'. For security reasons, you may have to have a police check first.

The Audit Commission Report outlines key training priorities for school staff identified by current SENCOs. These relate to core classroom skills and are ranked in order of priority:

- curriculum differentiation
- behaviour management
- target setting/writing and using IEPs
- SEN Code of Practice
- teaching literacy
- working with assistants/inclusive classrooms
- dyslexia/specific learning difficulties
- identifying needs/early identification
- general understanding of SEN
- speech and language difficulties
- working with other agencies.

Task 5

What are your own main concerns? List them in order of priority. Do they correspond with the priorities ranked here? What sort of training do you think should be provided to address these needs?

Personal tragedy or society's responsibility?

Given that, on average, schools identify one in five of all children as having some kind of special educational need, and one in 30 children as having needs that require additional external advice or support, then 'inclusive practice' seems a daunting task for those working in classrooms. However, these figures reflect the findings of the 1978 Warnock Report, which was the first attempt to measure numbers of children whose needs differ in some way from their peers. In other words, the situation is *not* a worsening one; there has not been an influx of pupils with special educational needs in our schools in recent years. Contrary to the opinions of some, the ethos of inclusive education has not driven huge swathes of 'difficult to teach' children into mainstream schools from some erstwhile 'elsewhere'. The inclusion of more children with higher levels of need has been gradual, with only a small reduction in the number of special school places available. The fact remains, however, that one in five pupils (1.9 million children in England and Wales, figure from Audit Commission 2002) are considered to have special educational needs and are *entitled* to equality of opportunity within our classrooms. The most horrifying aspect of this should not be how to deliver this entitlement, but that so many children have been largely low priority in the past. If, instead of difference we see diversity, and seek to develop our practices accordingly, then, by removing the barriers to learning faced by so many children, we will reduce the numbers of those labelled as 'SEN' for the first time since the counting of them began.

The National Curriculum and Standards for QTS emphasise the need for inclusive values and an inclusive ethos within schools, LEAs and education itself. Rather than an emphasis on individual learners and their personal problems, inclusion is about the rights of each and every child and the responsibilities that such a view places on the education system and those who choose to work within it.

That is not to say that educators and schools will be left to sink or swim in the face of inclusion. It is widely recognised that developing confidence and skills in schools is the key to making inclusion work. Schools and teachers should be supported in developing their skills, knowledge and experience to ensure that teaching a wide range of abilities is part of a teacher's repertoire, not a specialised 'add-on' to normal practice.

Inclusion is supported by legislation, guidance and international rights (the declaration on inclusive education issued by UNESCO following the world conference in Salamanca, Spain, in 1994 was endorsed by 92 governments around the world). However, educational inclusion will not be achieved by legislation and declarations alone. Inclusion also, sometimes, seems at odds with other policies and practices. In 1998 the government's Schools Standards and Frameworks Act retained SATs tests and league tables; and let us not forget that selection is still a common practice in many state schools.

Summary and key points

It is perhaps, then, pertinent to return to our opening question, what does inclusion mean? The Centre for Studies on Inclusive Education (2000) defines inclusion in education as:

> Involving the processes of increasing the participation of students in, and reducing their exclusion from, the cultures, curricula and communities of local schools . . . Inclusion is concerned with improving schools for staff as well as for students.

In this sense, understanding inclusion is as much about understanding our own attitudes, values and principles, and the foundations of these, as it is about classroom practices. Led by guidelines, documents, standards and legislation, those working in education may be required to deliver inclusion; but only with appropriate understanding, support, training, experience and opportunities for reflection will they become effective providers of, and believers in, inclusive education for children with special educational needs.

Questions to aid reflection

1 In what ways has the notion of 'special needs' changed over the years?
2 What do you understand by the term 'inclusion' in relation to children with special educational needs?
3 What do you see as the most important factors in supporting the process of developing inclusive practices in schools?

Annotated bibliography

Gross, J. (1996) *Special Educational Needs in the Primary School : A Practical Guide*, Buckingham: Open University Press.
  This is a very readable book which provides, as the title says, practical guidance for primary school practitioners. The text includes strategies, information and advice for use at school and classroom level to cater for the needs of a wide range of children.
Mittler, P. (2000) *Working Towards Inclusive Education: Social Contexts*, London: David Fulton Publishers.
  This text provides a contemporary overview of inclusion in both educational and social contexts. The key issues and challenges surrounding inclusion are clearly drawn out, and international perspectives provide a useful dimension.

Bibliography

Audit Commission (2002) *Special Educational Needs: A Mainstream Issue*, London: Audit Commission.

Centre for Studies in Inclusive Education (2000) *Index for Inclusion,* Bristol: CSIE.

Department for Education (1993) Special Educational Needs Code of Practice, London: HMSO.

Department for Education and Employment (1999) *The National Curriculum Handbook for Primary Teachers in England,* London: DfEE.

Department for Education and Skills (2001a) *Inclusive Schooling: Children with Special Educational Needs,* London: DfES.

Department for Education and Skills (2001b) *Special Educational Needs Code of Practice,* London: DfES.

Department for Education and Skills (2002) *Intervening Early,* London: DfES.

Department for Education and Skills and Teacher Training Agency (2002) *Qualifying to Teach: Professional Standards for Qualified Teacher Status and Requirements for Initial Teacher Training,* London: DfES.

Mittler, P. (2000) *Working Towards Inclusive Education: Social Contexts,* London: David Fulton Publishers.

Plowden Committee (1967) *Children and their Primary Schools* (the Plowden Report), London: HMSO.

Solity, J. (1991) Special Needs: a discriminatory concept?', *Educational Psychology in Practice* 7(1), 12–19.

Special Educational Needs Report of the Committee of Enquiry into the Education of Handicapped Children and Young People DES (1978) (the Warnock Report), London: HMSO.

Webb, L. (1967) *Children with Special Needs in the Infants' School*, London: Collins.

9 Managing Behaviour for Learning

Jenny Crisp and Sue Soan

Introduction

With the government's continuing commitment to social and academic inclusion, and the media-influenced perception that behaviour remains a key problem for educators, it is vital that behaviour conducive to developing social skills to enable learners to work together and effective learning is promoted in schools (DfES/QCA 1999). This chapter will consider the meaning and use of the terms 'behaviour management' and 'learning behaviour', highlighting the roles of the learners and educators. It will discuss the types of behaviour that cause educators most concern and will provide a broad framework of responses to these problem behaviours. You will also be provided with the opportunity to relate your own experiences and observations to the main behaviour theories that provide educators with an understanding of why various strategies or interventions are utilised.

By the end of this chapter you should have:

- a better understanding of what 'learning behaviour' and 'behaviour management' are;
- understood the roles of the educator and learner with regard to promoting positive learning behaviour;
- a better understanding of the four theoretical perspectives discussed: psychodynamic, cognitive-behavioural, behaviourist and eco-systemic;
- an awareness of the 'triangle of influence' and how theories can explain learning behaviour in school contexts;
- an understanding of the importance of promoting effective communication through supportive relationships.

Definition of terms

Behaviour

First, it is important to understand that 'behaviour is a function of the person and the context' (Long 2003). Behaviour always has a purpose, whether it is interpreted as appropriate or inappropriate and it is learned and determined by antecedents and consequences (ABC of behaviour – Antecedents, Behaviour and Consequences). This helps form a complete picture of what caused the behaviour, the behaviour itself and then what happened after the behaviour occurred. Unfortunately, in school contexts when behaviour is mentioned, educators tend to assume that it is a negative behaviour. Thus behaviours exhibited by learners in a school context do not just 'occur', but are a result of the learner's relationship with himself, with others and with the curriculum.

Behaviour management

Behaviour management is a term applied in educational settings to the managing of the classroom environment, the resources utilised and the curricula, in such a way that learners can access and engage with the curriculum. Additionally, due to the Statement of Inclusion and the social and academic aims of the National Curriculum (DfEE/QCA 1999), behaviour management in schools also includes the outcomes of the learner's ability to develop both social skills and positive outlooks for his future. However, training for behaviour management is frequently delivered in the context of Additional or Special Educational Needs (AEN/SEN), suggesting that it is 'additional to' the normal provision. It is not usually addressed as part of subject knowledge, again supporting the perception that behaviour management is a reactive process, confronted only if effective teaching and learning are disrupted. This separation of learning from behaviour can mean that educators adopt a fragmented or a 'control' mentality approach to behaviour management that can have an effect on learning and cause a breakdown in relationships. Educators may also make assumptions about academic ability based on the learner's behaviour which can again lead to a breakdown of relationships, poor self-esteem, underachievement, disaffection and even disruption.

Learning behaviour

Learning and behaviour should be linked via the term 'learning behaviour' in order to reduce perceptions that 'promoting learning' and 'managing behaviour' are separate issues.

(Powell and Tod 2003: 38)

Figure 9.1 illustrates a possible conceptual framework for understanding learning behaviour in a school context (Powell and Tod 2003). It is most important that the 'triangle of influence' that surrounds a learner is appropriate and supportive. The three most influential factors that affect any learner's ability to achieve are the relationship with himself, with others, including educators and other learners, and with the curriculum (Brofenbrenner 1979). 'Learning behaviour' is, however, still obviously linked by outside factors such as family, policies, the community and cultures and other agencies.

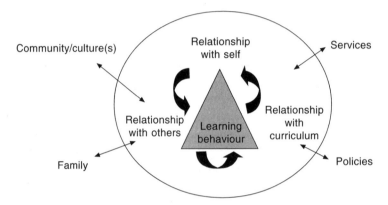

Figure 9.1 Behaviour management: inclusion (academic and social); attainment/ achievement and lifelong learning: conceptual framework

The way an individual feels about himself (self-esteem) is built up from early childhood experiences (Barrow *et al.* 2001). By interpreting the way others respond to him, the learner creates a view of himself that is directly interpreted from his perception of the way he has been treated. This is further set within a cultural framework where certain ideals are promoted as valuable and desirable. The greater the link between what the learner thinks of himself and his ideal of what he should be, the greater level of self-esteem will be established. However, learners often discover that their levels of esteem tend to fluctuate depending on the context and the situation they are in (Emler 2000).

For some learners, avoidance of certain curriculum areas is crucial to maintaining self-esteem and saving face, as they may be experiencing barriers to participating or achieving in a particular subject area. It is very important for educators to make efforts to understand 'how' and 'why' a learner behaves like he does in order to help him develop more appropriate behaviour.

Whole-school approach

Within our suggested 'triangle of influence' therefore it is essential that schools have a consistent, productive and supportive relationship with their learners. As Kaplan *et al.* (2002) state, educators 'need to construct learning environments in which school is thought of as a place where learning, understanding, improvement, and personal and social developments are valued and in which social comparison of a student's ability is de-emphasised'. Within this effective environment learners will be offered a place to enjoy purposeful activities, hence encouraging self-motivation. With sufficient motivation, a clear set of guidelines and suitable role models, learners will copy and adopt behaviours that enable them to become effective learners in the school context. This will develop independent learning skills and hence instigate the vehicle through which lifelong learning can be initiated.

Working collaboratively to encourage behaviour for learning

The impact of the way a whole school responds to a learner's difficulties should never be underestimated (Cooper *et al.* 2000). Many problematic situations can be solved, or at least improved, when school educators, parents and learner work together to alleviate the barrier(s) to learning. Implementing interventions and strategies based on one or more of the behavioural theories discussed and agreed by all involved will at least begin to focus attention on the areas of need. See Table 9.1.

It is also important to be aware that the subject matter we, as educators, communicate to a learner, will have an effect on his emotional state. Relationships between educator and learner are vital to promote appropriate learning behaviours, confidence and motivation in the classroom. Indeed, relationships and the learning environment in a school will contribute to, or reduce, the challenging behaviour of its learners (Thacker, *et al.* 2002). It is also important as educators to value each learner's achievement as opposed to developing competitive classroom cultures. Involving learners in the setting of their learning objectives gives them 'ownership' of targets and perhaps even more accurate judgements of their own performance. This is not a new strategy, but it can develop the relationship between educator and learner establishing an ethos of mutual respect and can 'contribute to improved confidence and self-image' (DfES 2001: 3:14).

Table 9.1   Behavioural theories

Frequent behaviour	Theory	Explanation	Action
Off-task	Behaviourist	Child is getting more attention by being off-task	Reward on-task behaviour
Off-task	Congnitive–behaviourist	Child thinks he is unable to do the task	Encourage child to re-appraise task: identify what parts of the task he can do, etc.
Off-task	Psychodynamic	Child fears failure	Circle time to build self-esteem – offer increased adult or peer support
Off-task	Eco-systemic	'He has a brother who is just the same'	Possibly nurture group or work with parents

Source: Adapted from Tod (forthcoming)

Task 1

Think of a situation in which you were involved in dealing with a learner's difficult behaviour. How were you, as the educator, and the learner supported by the whole-school systems and policies? If there were areas of concern, how could these be improved using the information above?

What types of behaviour cause educators most concern?

Research for a DfEE (Department for Education and Employment, now DfES) survey published in 1989 found that educators of both primary and secondary pupils agreed on a range of behaviours that they found particularly irritating. Some 70 per cent cited answering back and use of offensive language as the top problem, with 80 per cent of respondents stating that this occurred on a regular basis. Some of the other key problem areas mentioned were talking out of turn, calculated idleness, hindering others who are working and unnecessary verbal noise. A single such behaviour is not problematic, but, when frequent and intense, it can become inappropriate for the learning context. For some educators the disruption generated by this type of behaviour can engender feelings of anger, stress and anxiety. If the behaviours continue, there is also the possibility that other learners will begin to experience raised levels of anxiety. If this occurs, the teaching–learning process will be interrupted and the learning environment will feel insecure and unsafe. At this stage it may be necessary to examine 'learning behaviour' as a whole-school issue.

Task 2

Observe a lesson in your workplace. Record all behaviours you see that support the smooth running of the classroom. Concurrently also record all the incidents of behaviour that disrupt learning. Note down how often they occur and, if you are able to, track what happened just before and just after each incident (ABC of Behaviour). Try not to interpret the events, merely observe what happens.

A broad framework from which to respond to problematic behaviours

How an educator responds to interruptions that adversely affect the efficient education of learners is vital. It is desirable that the situation is brought to a successful conclusion by avoiding a position where one person has to win at the expense of the other. For example, suppose an educator takes an overbearing stance to a learner's refusal to remove his cap by shouting and physically being confrontational by standing directly in front of him. There is a danger of placing the learner in a position where conforming to the educator's request would make him 'lose face' in front of his peer group. At the same time failure to get the learner to comply could cause the educator to 'lose face'.

Task 3

Take a few minutes to reflect on a situation in the past where you think this type of incident took place. Who became involved? Why? How was the situation resolved and how did the other learners and educators respond to the situation?

Another educator in a similar situation with a learner remains calm and positive and follows through the implementation of the school's agreed response for such behaviour. In this scenario there is a greater possibility of a positive outcome because the educator controlled the response to the learner's behaviour in a professional and non-confrontational manner. This highlights the importance of the nature and type of action taken by educators who have regular contact with learners. A wide variety of sources are available to support educators which provide written or visual illustration of appropriate approaches designed to deal with particular issues (Cowley 2000: Rogers 2000).

Rob Long (2003) also draws attention to the fact that it is important for educators to focus on dealing with primary behaviours rather than on the follow-on secondary ones. The following is an example of a successful management of a primary behaviour. A learner is chewing gum. This is the primary behaviour since the class rule forbids chewing gum. When asked by the educator to spit the gum into the waste bin, the child sulks and calls out a rude response. This is a secondary behaviour. The educator remains focused on the primary behaviour and while keeping voice level and calm repeats the instruction to put the gum in the bin with a clear 'thank you'. If the learner chooses not to comply, the appropriate school sanction will be followed through. Thus the primary behaviour is dealt with without disrupting the lesson or other learners.

Task 4

Take another look at the incident you thought about for Task 3. With hindsight, what changes of attitude or behaviour from anyone involved do you feel may have had the potential to achieve a more positive outcome?

Reframing responses according to the main behavioural theories

How do theories explain learning behaviour in school contexts? In this section of the chapter you will be introduced to four behavioural theories and their importance for educators in a school context. Knowing about these theories is important because whatever type of responses schools and educators take regarding behaviour for learning, they need to have an understanding of why and for what purpose they are responding to learners' behaviour in certain ways. It may also shed light on why certain strategies are used in your educational setting. However, it must be acknowledged that in practice interventions for learners with behavioural difficulties are usually adopted due to the common sense of the educator or on past school experience, not on any evaluated effectiveness (Olsen and Cooper 2001). The theories we are going to examine are:

- psychodynamic theory;
- behaviourist theory;
- cognitive–behaviourist theory;
- eco-systemic theory.

Using Table 9.1 as an example, it is possible to see how one particular behaviour, 'off-task' can be 'managed' in different ways according to the needs of the learner.

Psychodynamic theory

This is an approach that is closely associated with socio-biology, psychology and psychiatry, each of which stresses the biological and evolutionary foundations of human behaviour. 'Psychodynamic' is a term used when discussing the study of interacting motives and emotions. When working 'psychodynamically' in a school context, it is frequently the 'Attachment Theory' developed by John Bowlby that is actually being implemented. This is based on psychodynamic theory, (and also on Control Theory and Ethology) and is:

> a theory about relationships, based on the idea that human beings evolved in kinship groups and that in the original 'environment of evolutionary adaptedness' (Bowlby 1969) survival was increased by the maintenance of secure bonds between their members, primarily, but by no means exclusively, between parents and children.
>
> (Holmes 1995: 178–9)

According to this perspective, how learners feel about themselves can determine how they behave. Past experiences, as well as current ones, shape how learners feel as they seek to make sense of their world. For example, if a learner keeps distracting others and avoids completing his own work, it might be that he has developed this behaviour because he feels he is going to fail in the set task. Therefore why complete a task that is going to gain a negative response from the educator? Another example of this is when a learner has completed a 'good' piece of work and the educator praises his efforts and results. In response to the praise, the learner tears up the work and becomes sad or angry. Perhaps this behaviour illustrates to the educator that the learner has such low self-worth that they are unable to accept or even acknowledge that anything they do is adequate, let alone 'good' – in fact, they are not a 'good' person. As educators we need to keep in mind that there may be unknown explanations for the behaviour of the learner, as the 'triangle of influence' illustrated earlier in the chapter (Figure 9.1). These external influences may be beyond the control of the school context, but, by adopting a psychodynamic approach, the emphasis of the intervention as a means to encourage 'behaviour for learning' would be on understanding the origins of the behaviour from the learner's perspective and seeking ways to minimise the barriers to learning. Such learners may be a 'looked after' child or a member of a 'family under stress' and as a consequence are unable emotionally to take full advantage of the available learning experiences. In this type of situation, a whole-school approach including collaborative working with outside agencies and carers, as discussed earlier, is vital if appropriate behaviour for learning is to be achieved.

Behaviourist theory

Behaviour theorists like Wheldall, Watson and Skinner (cited in Olsen and Cooper 2001) state that the most effective way to help learners is to teach them new behaviours by using rewards and sanctions. Thus, a learner will be rewarded for appropriate behaviour, but sanctioned for any inappropriate behaviour. The philosophy supporting this theoretical approach encompasses the reasoning that rewards and sanctions are the most powerful means of shaping behaviour. Decisions regarding the implementation of rewards or sanctions are made following the observation, documentation and analysis of the relevant behaviour. For example, a child who has difficulties in the playground, often hitting the other children, will be closely observed. The number of times the child hits others will be recorded and a programme of intervention will be designed for him. The child will be rewarded for the number of playtimes during which others are not hit and sanctions and the withdrawal of privileges are applied when hitting does occur. The belief behind this approach is that the rewards will reinforce and shape the desired behaviour, while at the same time making the negative behaviour less attractive. It is useful to know that behavioural approaches tend to underpin classroom management strategy and most school discipline policies.

However, a number of theorists felt that the 'behaviourist' approach illustrated was very restrictive. For example Vygotsky, Piaget and Bruner (for further details, see Chapter 1) all expressed their concerns, stating that learning was an active (social constructivist) process. They felt educators needed to take account of the social situation in which the behaviour occurred. They promoted the idea expressed at the beginning of this chapter, that behaviour does not occur in a vacuum, but is very dependent on the specific context in which it happens and the involvement of others (cited in Olsen and Cooper 2001).

Cognitive-behaviourist theory

Cognitive theorists such as Seligman (1990) believe that learners who display emotional and behavioural difficulties need to be helped to develop different ways of thinking about situations, of encouraging actual change in their perceptions. It is thought possible to alter a learner's behaviour by teaching him to think or perceive things differently.

In undertaking a cognitive approach, the educator would encourage the learner to engage in a process of analysis and redirect his attention towards other ways of thinking and looking at things. Take the case of Peter who was teased every day in the playground. What was Peter's perception of the situation? He felt that all the other children hated him because of the regularity of the teasing. He was told and encouraged to understand that teasing was happening to other children on a regular basis as well, and that he was not the only one being teased. He learned that just because someone teased you, it did not necessarily mean they hated you. As a consequence of this, he was taught to manage his feelings in the light of the information and understanding he had gained. For example, he could accept the feeling that when he was teased he felt sad, but he didn't have to respond, perhaps even physically, to the feeling that they hated him.

Eco-systemic theory

The eco-systemic theory primarily follows the ideas of the behaviourists and is concerned with the effect of the environment on the learner. Eco-systemic theorists like Olson and Cooper (2001) support the view that learners displaying social, emotional and behavioural difficulties are doing so in a direct response to the environment. They understand that behaviours do not occur in isolation, but as a result of the relationship the learner has with self, with others and with the curriculum. This approach differs from the other theories discussed in this chapter because interventions implemented do not involve the teaching of new skills to the learner by the educator. It is the contributory factors to the behaviour, such as the school policies and the procedures and methods of communication that are examined. It incorporates the (constructivist) view of coming to a shared understanding as a means of moving forward in a positive way. The aim of this type of investigation is to create an environment whereby high expectations and positive relationships encourage successful learning to take place with minimal distractions and maximum cooperation. If this is related to Table 9.1 where the educators are seeking reasons to explain 'off-task' behaviour, an intervention following this theory may include the establishment of a 'circle of friends' group, or a nurture group or might result in a request for a medical assessment. It would also perhaps suggest more suitable learning challenges within the classroom, removing any unwarranted levels of anxiety or stress for the learner, while at the same time supporting the learner to reach his full potential.

Task 5

Look back at the notes you made for the previous tasks. Identify a behaviour problem of a particular learner and then use your knowledge of the theories mentioned above to help you plan an effective intervention.

Summary and key points

You should have gained an understanding of the theoretical perspectives discussed in this chapter and their importance when considering responses to situations in which the educator needs to promote behaviour for learning. As you have read, there are a wide range of strategies used by educators to 'manage' learners' behaviours, each one fashioned by personal philosophies and attitudes. It should be clear, therefore, that educators need to 'know' the learners and have constructive relationships with them. However, it is also vital that they have underpinning knowledge and an understanding of the theoretical perspectives in order to respond appropriately to less desirable behaviour, to promote the development of attitudes that nurture and encourage appropriate behaviour for learning.

With all this in mind, the main points to remember from this chapter can be given as the following memory aids: relationships, responsibility and relevance.

Relationships

It is essential to build strong relationships based on mutual respect alongside attitudes that encourage and support, rather than diminish and devalue.

Responsibility

'Behaving to learn' is a shared responsibility. The learner needs to be supported and encouraged by the guidelines and examples demonstrated to him by the educators and the whole-school environment, in order to develop responsibility for his own behaviour. The responsibility for 'behaving to learn' does finally rest with the individual learner, but it must not be forgotten that the learner is influenced immensely by the attitudes and treatment received from the educators.

Relevance

Finally, the curriculum and other learning experiences need to be relevant and appropriate to the ability and aptitude of the learner. When additional or different support is required, it is the responsibility of the whole school to respond in consistent and positive ways.

With this underpinning understanding of theories and awareness of the importance of relationships, responsibility and relevance, you will be able to work together with learners to create not only positive educational experiences for all, but behaviour for learning that fosters a desire for lifelong learning.

Questions to aid reflection

1 How might your understanding of behavioural theories help in developing your classroom practice?
2 What do you consider to be your role in assisting learners in developing more appropriate learning behaviour?
3 Do you know which theoretical perspectives are adopted and utilised in your educational setting?
4 Do the policies in your school setting reflect shared understanding in promoting effective learning behaviour? Do the policies reflect actual school practice?

Annotated bibliography

The Association of Workers with Emotional and Behavioural Difficulties publishes journals to give current updates on behavioural and environmental issues. Questionnaires to assess the social and emotional status of children can also be ordered through this association.

Kaplan, A., Gheen, M. and Midgley, C. (2002) 'Classroom goal structure and student disruptive behaviour', *British Journal of Educational Psychology*, 72: 191–211.

Loomans, D. and Loomans, J. (1994) *Full Esteem Ahead*. Reading, MA: Allyn & Bacon.

Tiburon, H., Kramer, J., Canfield, J. and Wells, H.C. (1994) *100 Ways to Enhance Self-Concept in the Classroom*, 2nd edn, Reading, MA: Allyn & Bacon.

Just as the two titles above suggest, these books are both packed with excellent ideas for raising the regard children have for themselves.

Rogers, B. (2000) *Classroom Behaviour: A Practical Guide to Effective Classroom Behaviour*, London: Books Education.

This book provides useful strategies and techniques for practitioners to instantly use and rehearse with children and young people. It will help you to set up appropriate rules and boundaries and explains how to maintain them with dignity.

Websites

www.behaviouruk.com

Promoting citizenship, this company markets a very interesting and effective interactive 'Conduct File' which can be used with individual children or educators requiring inspiration for PSHE lessons. It is a tried and tested programme that is designed to encourage learners at both primary and secondary level to develop self-regulating behaviour.

http://sesilnet.uiuc.edu

Contains a wide range of information to help readers to overcome adversity.

http://education.cant.ac.uk/xplanatory

A most informative site offering links to articles, presentations, tutorials for educators seeking help for learners experiencing difficulties with school.

Bibliography

Barrow, G., Bradshaw, E. and Newton, T. (2001) *Improving Behaviour and Raising Self-Esteem in the Classroom: A Practical Guide to Using Transactional Analysis,* London: David Fulton Publishers.

Bowlby, J. (1969) *Attachment and Loss*, Vol. 1. *Separation,* London: Hogarth Press.

Brofenbrenner, E. (1979) *The Ecology of Human Development: Experiments by Nature and Design*, Cambridge: MA: Harvard University Press.

Clements, J. and Zarkowska, E. (1994) *Problem Behaviour in People with Severe Learning Disabilities: The STAR Approach*, London: Chapman and Hall.

Cooper, P., Drummond, M.J., Hart, S., Lovey, J. and McLaughlin, C. (2000) *Positive Alternatives to Exclusion,* London: RoutledgeFalmer.

Cowley, S. (2000) *Getting the Buggers to Behave,* London: Continuum.

DfES (2001) *Special Educational Needs: Code of Practice*, London: HMSO.

DfEE/QCA (1999) *The National Curriculum for England,* London: HMSO.

Emler, N. (2000) *Self-Esteem: The Costs and Causes of Low Self-Worth*, York: The Rowntree Foundation.

Holmes, J. (1995) *John Bowlby and Attachment Theory*, London: Routledge.

Kaplan, A., Gheen, M. and Midgley, C. (2002) 'Classroom goal structure and student disruptive behaviour', *British Journal of Educational Psychology*, 72: 191–211.

Long, R. (2003) Quotation taken at a NASEN conference held at Canterbury Christ Church University College.

Mosley, J. (1996) *Quality Circle Time*, Cambridge: LDA.

Olsen, J. and Cooper, P. (2001) *Dealing with Disruption in the Classroom*, London: Kogan Page.

Powell. S. and Tod, J. (forthcoming) 'EPPI Systematic Literature Review: Behaviour Management'.

Rogers, B. (2000) *Classroom Behaviour: A Practical Guide to Effective Classroom Behaviour,* London: Books Education.

Thacker, J. Strudwick, D. and Babbedge, E. (2002) *Educating Children with Emotional and Behavioural Difficulties: Inclusive Practice in Mainstream Schools,* London: Routledge/Falmer, cited in Powell, S. and Tod, J. (forthcoming) 'EPPI Systematic Review: Behaviour Management'.

Seligman, M. (1990) *Learned Optimism,* New York: Pocket Books.

Gender Issues in Education

Guy Roberts-Holmes

Introduction

The social construction of gender is a powerful aspect of all our identities. This chapter will help you to understand more about some of the complex gendering processes occurring within your educational institution. Our understandings of boys and girls, men and women have, for some, undergone a radical transformation in recent times and as you read this chapter you may wish to reflect critically upon the various ways in which your own lives are deeply gendered.

The term sex difference is used to refer to the biological differences between boys and girls and men and women. Gender difference refers to the socially constructed categories and meanings built upon the biological differences between the sexes. Gender also refers to the social identity of being male or female and is learned through social experiences. Nowadays this gendering process can sometimes begin even before the baby is born. Parents who know the sex of their forthcoming baby may buy gender-specific toys and clothing and build up gendered expectations and feelings. 'A baby cannot but swim in a sea of gendered discourses, already in place at the time of the child's birth, for gender is one of our primary ways of making sense of the world' (Epstein *et al.* 1998: 60).

The complex and ongoing process of 'gendering' continues through babyhood and early childhood. Gender can become institutionally confirmed through the processes of schooling.

Gender stereotypes are firm beliefs about what women and men, boys and girls are 'naturally' like in behaviour, talents or weaknesses. Gender stereotypes are commonly held within society and are very powerful and difficult to challenge, especially for children. Indeed, gender is one of the primary categories by which we organise our social world.

By the end of this chapter you should have:

- become aware that the social and cultural construction of gender is powerful and difficult for girls and boys to challenge;
- understood that the process of schooling itself can inadvertently contribute to stereotypical gendered behaviour;
- considered the ways in which a person's gender, 'race' and class are intertwined;
- understood that a learner's gender is not as significant as class in predicting educational attainment.

Gender stereotypes and the Victorian legacy

Today's gender stereotypes can be seen as originating in Victorian values held about the supposedly 'natural' differences between men and women. The Victorians saw sex-based differences as holding specific male and female social characteristics and abilities. The male and female gendered characteristics were constructed in opposition and dualism to each other, succinctly put by the Victorian poet Tennyson,

> Man for the Field and Woman for the Hearth:
> Man for the Sword and for the Needle She:
> Man with the Head and Woman with the Heart:
> Man to command and Woman to obey:
> All else confusion.
>
> (Tennyson, The Princess, 1847, quoted in Paetcher 1998: 8)

The ideal middle-class Victorian woman was constructed as a mother who stayed at home to look after *her* children and was a housewife. The Victorian popular view was that women were different from and inferior to men, not only biologically but socially, intellectually and psychologically (Arnot *et al.* 1999). In contrast, the ideal Victorian man was constructed by the Victorians as rational, logical and unemotional and worked outside of the home in the public domain. Indeed, the Victorians felt that it was potentially dangerous to encourage a woman's intellect since this might harm her 'natural' childbearing and rearing abilities. 'The possession of womb was thought to render a woman unfit for deep thought, which might tax her reproductive powers or make her less amenable to rearing children' (Walderdine 1990: 22, in Arnot *et al.* 1999: 37). These strongly held Victorian values and beliefs were challenged in the twentieth century as women gradually acquired full civil rights. However, the Victorian legacies can be seen to operate within the employment of men and women within the education sector.

Gender and education employment

Women outnumber men in the teaching profession, making up over three-quarters of the teachers in primary schools and just under half of the teachers in secondary schools. Although numerically women far outweigh men in the primary sector, men are more likely to become head teachers than women. Indeed one male primary teacher in four is a head teacher, whereas the chances of becoming a female head teacher is one in thirteen. The result of more men in positions of authority in primary schools means that they tend to earn more than women on average.

As the age of the pupils increases, so the proportion of women teachers decreases. Within nursery and infant schools 91 per cent of the staff are female. This is in part due to the historical construction of the nursery/infant class as a 'substitute home' with a substitute mother caring for the young children. The supposed 'natural qualities' of women with young children, and that men who work with young children are sometimes perceived as either principals in training or paedophiles has helped to retain this massive gender imbalance. Interestingly in the Further and Higher Education sectors, where the students are older, men still far outnumber women especially in senior posts. Within the more prestigious older universities there are approximately three men to every woman at lecturer level, almost nine men to every woman at senior lecturer level and just over 19 men to every woman at the level of professor. This discrepancy is particularly great in the sciences and mathematics, where male lecturers outnumber females by seven to one and male professors outnumber females by 53 to one. Currently only 6 per cent of professors are women.

Task 1

The following questions are about the ways in which gender may have affected your career. These questions can be reflected upon on your own and then, if you wish, discussed with others.

Why are male teachers so under-represented within the early years and primary schools?

What can be done to encourage male teachers in the early years and primary sectors?

The Nature/Nurture debate

The Nature/Nurture debate examines the extent to which a girl's or a boy's behaviour is affected by biology or sociology. The Nature side of the debate states that girls and boys have a different biological and hormonal make-up which predisposes boys and girls to act in different ways. At the extreme end of this argument, biology is deemed to explain all the differences between the sexes at school and in society. For the biological determinist, gender differences and inequalities are 'natural' and are an inevitable and unchangeable part of a 'natural order'. At the other extreme, the Nurture proponents argue that society's different expectations and attitudes towards boys and girls are the sole reason for differences in their behaviour. The Nurture proponents believe that gender is a social and cultural construction which varies according to history, geographical location and culture. Thus, they would point out that the expectations, attitudes and behaviour for some girls and women today are radically different from that in the past because the social construction of what it means to be a girl/woman has for some dramatically changed. The Nature/Nurture debate is far from settled and arguments rage concerning the relative importance of one or the other. It would seem that both sides of the argument have some validity.

The Nature/Biological argument

Biological determinists argue that the differing behaviour and interests commonly seen between boys and girls are reducible to biology. Recent brain research suggests that neuronal connections are selectively strengthened as a result of experience and thus differential experience will lead to differences in neural connections. Men and women experience the world in different ways because of their different bodies and positions in society, hence these experiences are likely to have an influence on the ways in which their brains function (Paetcher 1998: 46). Some female brains, it is believed, are better organised and connected for language and emotional development than some male brains because this has been the female gendered experience from birth; their brain development has followed their gendered identity. Equally, the chemical testosterone produced predominately by men can tend to make them more competitive because the brain might be responding to the stereotypical male gendered identity of competitiveness. However, biological determinism does not have an explanation for why there are as many differences within the category of boys and within the category of girls as there are differences between boys and girls. Thus some boys may have behaviour which is more closely associated with girls' stereotypical behaviour, while some girls may have behaviour which is more closely associated with boys' stereotypical behaviour. Some commentators have argued that children's identity may be limited by constraining them to gender stereotypes. 'No group of children or any individual should be essentialised – in other words, defined and bound within this definition as if it were impossible for any individual to escape this' (Siraj-Blatchford and Clarke 2000: 12).

The Nurture/Socialisation argument

The advocates of the Nurture debate, known as the socialisation theorists, argue that children are actively encouraged to learn their genders and normal gendered behaviour from birth. As soon as a baby is born, people want to know if it is a boy or a girl and the ways in which this information is responded to is based on a whole set of social and cultural assumptions about that baby's gendered future. People assume that these social and cultural assumptions about the baby's gender will follow fairly automatically from the physical ones (Paetcher 1998: 38).

The following experiment (Lloyd 1987; Channel 4 2001) shows the highly differentiated ways in which language, expectations, attitudes and behaviour are predicated upon supposed biological differences. The experiment of dressing up a baby boy in pink and then in blue and recording different carer's language and expectations is most revealing. When the baby is presented dressed in pink, some carers use female stereotypical behaviour. Carers praise the baby 'girl' for being 'pretty, beautiful and lovely' and suggest that this 'girl' might grow up to become a beautician! Their tone is gentle and soft. However, when the same carers are presented with the baby dressed in blue, they tend to use male gender stereotypical language: 'What a big boy, look how strong you are' and suggest that when he grows up the baby boy might be 'a big policeman or a footballer'! The carers' tone tended to be rougher and more robust than with the girl baby. Interestingly, some of the carers also hold the baby in different ways depending upon whether they think the baby is a boy or a girl. Thus, when dressed in pink, they closely held the baby 'girl' gently rocking 'her'. Baby boys tended to be held further away from them and handled more roughly. In public spaces carers tend to allow greater physical freedom for boy toddlers than for girl toddlers. Thus, boys are allowed to go further away from their carers than girls before being picked up and brought back. Such differentiated behaviour on the part of carers/parents may be based upon assumed differences between the genders. Any such difference is certainly reinforced by the carer/parent. The above experiments support the view that the way a child is reared is a key factor in determining gender identity.

Thus, there is evidence to suggest that some carers and their families and friends repeat over and over again, every day, that their babies and toddlers are either 'pretty girls' or 'big strong boys'. This consistent labelling process and subtle physical caring differences can become internalised by young children. Carers tend to dress boys and girls differently and gender stereotypical toys can reinforce this gendering process.

Imitation of same-sex family role models

Boys and girls tend to identify with and imitate same-sex role models within their families. Children's imitation of the gendered behaviour of family members whom they love can be a very powerful source of learning for children. This is clearly not always the case but there is a tendency for imitation along gendered lines. Such gendered behaviour may be copied by the children and thus become learned and possibly re-enacted. Some fathers and mothers will have stereotypical and traditional work and home patterns of behaviour, however, increasingly families may have more contemporary gendered patterns of behaviour.

Gendered toys, books and media role models

Task 2

Everyone has opinions about some of the toys they think children should play with, whether they admit to them or not. Look at the pictures from a recent toy catalogue.

Do you agree or disagree with this sort of advertising for children's toys? Can you explain why you agree or disagree? What sort of play do you think is encouraged for girls and for boys by the toy advertisements?

Boys are encouraged to play with toys which generally favour gross motor skills and vigorous activity while girls tend to be encouraged with more gentle play things. Racing cars, dinosaurs, and Action Men figures tend to encourage aggressive and dominating language and play styles. Soft dolls and animals and dressing-up clothes tend to encourage gentle language and play styles. Research has shown that from an early age young girls are given more opportunities and encouraged to talk about their feelings. Boys, on the other hand, tend to be encouraged to hide their feelings and might even be told that 'big boys don't cry'. Even when carers do not overtly tell children which toys to select and play with, they demonstrate their approval by praising and engaging with the child's play if they feel the child has selected a gender-appropriate toy. Thus by the age of one some baby boys and girls have been shown to have differentiated toy choice and play styles. Children's literature and children's TV can sometimes encourage a gendered approach to emotions with very powerful gender-stereotypical role models. There are considerably more all-action male superheroes than females who tend to play subordinate and secondary roles to the lead male characters. All of the above social processes continuously reinforce gender differentiation. Children may thus build up differentiated gender categories and assign themselves to one or other of the categories and act out the gender stereotypes, possibly being encouraged and praised for doing so.

Task 3

Analyse the children's books that are in your workplace. Look at the visual images they show of male and female roles. Who are the central characters and what role are they playing? What sort of activities are females and males shown to be doing? See if you can find some books that you would recommend, that show both females and males in positive non-stereotypical roles.

Children actively 'policing' each other's gender

It is important to note that children do not simply passively absorb such gender differentiation but rather are active themselves within this process.

Task 4

Children are playing 'hospitals' in the home corner. A boy announces that he is going to be the doctor and tells his friend, 'You're a girl so you have to be the nurse.' How will you deal with this situation?

Some children and their carers challenge and rework stereotypical gender codes. The desire to have power encourages some girls to dress and play with clothes more usually associated with boys. Thus, 'for a girl, being more boyish means being more powerful in the world. For a boy to be more female is to be less powerful' (Epstein 1998: 59).

Equally, boys may understand that to dress with girls' clothes and play with girls' toys is less powerful and therefore less desirable than boys' clothes and toys. This perhaps explains why it is rarer to see boys 'crossing over' into girls' clothes and toys than for some girls to cross over into boy's clothes and activities. Indeed, some carers/parents are proud of their girls being 'tomboys', whereas this is very rarely the case with boys who are more effeminate. However, some boys in certain 'safe' contexts are interested in toys and activities more usually associated with girls and will enact more feminine storylines out. Thus, when encouraged, boys will play with dolls, doll houses, soft toys and use gentle language and storylines. Thus, at home with supportive and encouraging carers a boy may play with dolls. However, such behaviour may not be tolerated by other boys and girls in the more public space of the nursery or school.

Within a school context, boys who engage with feminine stereotypical play may make themselves vulnerable to teasing by other boys and girls. Moreover, carers may not approve of their male offspring engaging in supposedly female activities. Thus, for boys to engage in so-called feminine activities in anyway may be potentially problematic. Mac An Ghail (1994) has written that 'schools operate as masculine making devices' and Epstein has noted that schools are 'particularly difficult places for boys to depart from the norm' (1998: 12). Hence the processes of schooling itself may constrain and limit identity possibilities for both girls and boys. Children can punish those whose behaviours are perceived as being not sufficiently masculine or feminine. The following are real-life case studies in which boys and girls actively 'policed' their own and each other's gendered behaviour. Such 'policing' attempts to regulate children's gendered 'norms' and parameters.

Case Study I

> Researcher: Pippa, lots of the time I see the girls playing in the home corner. Is there some special reason for that?
> Pippa: Yes, because they like playing mothers.
> Researcher: What do they like about that?
> Pippa: Well, I like going there and feeding the babies in the pram.
> Researcher: What about the boys, do they ever play mothers?
> Pippa: Sam always plays. He's always playing mum.
> Researcher: Does he? So do you play with Sam much?
> Pippa: No.
> Researcher: Why not?
> Pippa: I don't want to because I don't like him.
> Researcher: Why don't you like him Pippa?
> Pippa: Because he always says lots of hard things to me.

'The 'hard things' that Pippa referred to were Sam's regular demands to be "mum" in the home corner and to wear the glittery skirt that "mum" did. Sam often told Pippa she was "not fair"' (MacNaughton 2000: 106).'

In the above case study, Pippa enjoys acting out being a mum with other girls. Pippa actively challenges Sam's behaviour and encourages him to move away from what she perceives as 'girls-only play'. Pippa is thus preventing a boy in his attempts to question stereotypical gender boundaries and act out different ways of being a boy.

Case Study 2

What is going on in the following real-life case study? (MacNaughton 2000: 106).

> Researcher: Are there any places in the nursery that you don't play?
> Pippa: I don't like playing with the blocks.
> Researcher: Why not?
> Pippa: Because I like to go higher and higher but then they (*pointing to the boys*) smash them down and hurt my ears.

In this case study it was the turn of the boys to keep Pippa away from an activity which they perceived as being for 'boys only'. The boys were attempting to control the brick building area for themselves and were prepared to physically destroy a girl's attempt at crossing over stereotypical gendered boundaries. The above small real-life examples illustrate the subtle and complex ways in which children within institutions can confirm gendered identities.

Task 5

What do you think is going on in the following real-life story?

Jake and the soft pink rabbit

Jake, a five-year-old boy, had been playing at home with a soft, pink rabbit he called 'Thumper'. Jake decided to take him to school in his jacket pocket. In his other jacket pocket Jake had a Spiderman. As Jake was walking across the playground to the classroom on the following morning, he stopped, unzipped his pocket took out Thumper and quietly said to his father;

Jake: Put him in the car now Daddy.
Dad: Why?
Jake: You know.
Dad: Yes, I'll put him in the car, but why?
Jake: Cos, I play with Spiderman *here.*

In what ways does Jake show his understandings that there are different ways to be a boy dependent upon the context?

   What do you think other boys and girls would have said if Jake had played with Thumper in the playground?

   What do you think other boys and girls will say to Jake with his Spiderman?

The historical academic attainments of girls and boys

In the 1950s and 1960s girls had to do better than boys to obtain a grammar school place. Girls who obtained higher than average scores than boys sometimes had their scores adjusted downwards otherwise grammar schools would have been overwhelmingly populated by girls (Epstein *et al.* 1998). This practice was informed by the then prevalent ideologies that 'boys develop later than girls' and that boys have 'innate intellectual potential'. This fiction of all boys' innate intellectual potential has historically protected boys' underachievement from scrutiny and any academic success has been related to this mythologised 'innate potential'. These ideologies of the innately intelligent boy directly influenced educational policy during the 1940s and 1950s. Since boys were supposedly late developers with innate potential, it was felt unfair to compare directly boys and girls academic attainments. Hence, a policy of positive discrimination in favour of boys was widely adopted throughout the education system with a 'technical adjustment' at 11+ in favour of the boys. This, coupled with an historic shortage of girls' grammar school places, served to obfuscate the historical higher attainment of girls. Hence, there is nothing new in the fact that some girls have historically achieved higher attainment than some boys. What is new is that this attainment gap in favour of girls is now clearly visible and this achievement gap is increasing (Gillborn and Mizra 2000). When boys academically fail, this has been attributed to teachers, teaching methods, books, biology, different learning styles – indeed, anything other than implicating the boys themselves! Interestingly, when girls fail, this has historically been explained by something within – their poor intellectual capability, whereas when they succeed this was due to something external – female teachers, teaching methods, assessment procedures or particular conditions (Cohen 1998).

The contemporary 'Gender Gap' in attainment

In 1989, 29.8 per cent of boys and 35.8 per cent of girls attained five or more A*–C, GCSE passes, a gap of six percentage points: by 1999, however, the gap had increased to more than eleven points, with 43 per cent of white boys and 55 per cent of white girls attaining five A*–C grades. This gender gap varies depending upon class and 'race' issues (see discussion below). A gender gap in favour of girls has recently been noted in grade As at 'A'-levels and girls now outperform boys in 'A'-level sciences and maths as well as the humanities. Interestingly, a gender gap is noticeable within all ethnic groups so that Indian girls outperform Indian boys and African-Caribbean girls outperform African-Caribbean boys. Additionally, a 'moral panic' about boys' attainment has occurred in other countries too, so that the debate is now international.

The reasons for this increasing gender gap are complex and research has pointed to a variety of factors such as:

- the introduction of comprehensive schools and the ending of the 11+ (in some counties);
- new assessment procedures (such as SATs) and the competitive school league tables so that gendered academic performance is now much more visible than before;
- the positive impact of targeted equal opportunities for girls;
- the introduction of the National Curriculum in which all pupils had to take a balanced cluster of subjects (in 1988, 42 per cent of girls took home economics whereas in 1993, only 15 per cent of girls took home economics);
- a transformation in gender relations, expectations and attitudes throughout society;
- the different ways in which masculinity and femininity are constructed within schools.

> *Task 6*
>
> Note down all the changes that have occurred in gender stereotypes, expectations and attitudes in our society in the past 50 years. In what ways do you think these social and cultural changes have impacted upon boys and girls expectations of themselves at school?

The construction of masculinity and femininity in schools

Boys learn to dissociate themselves from girls at an early age by engaging in a process known as 'Othering'. This process of othering may occur because young children's gender may be learned through understanding what they are not (Siraj-Blatchford and Clarke 2000). Young boys may have very negative reactions to stereotypical girl toy advertisements such as Barbies. Some feminists argue that, equally, young boys may be picking up patriarchal messages in society that can serve to devalue girls and women. Othering involves a process of dualism and opposition such as described earlier in the ideal Victorian woman who stays at home and looks after the children and the man who is outside 'working'.

Within a school this feminine/masculine division can occur over school and school work. An academic/non-academic couplet can become associated with a female/male division such that to be academic is part of being a girl and to be non-academic is part of being a boy. 'In many traditional, macho, boys' cultures, school learning is effeminised. Some boys' hardness and adequacy as "real lads" is deliberately formed in relation to a sissified world of school work' (Jackson 1998: 89).

Some boys even go so far as to fail at academic work in order to protect their vulnerable masculinity because academic achievement is perceived as effeminate. In a recent television documentary a boy was asked 'What would you think of a boy who worked hard at school?' to which the boy replied without hesitation, 'He's not a boy' (Epstein *et al.* 1998: 96). This captures the essence of the problem for some boys. The difficulty for some boys in some contexts is to negotiate being 'cool' with success at academic work. Hence, successfully doing school work and holding on to a tough 'male' image is a difficult identity for some boys to negotiate. Since academic success for some boys is so closely connected with being a girl, academic success becomes problematic for some boys because working hard at school makes them vulnerable to the accusation of being a girl. One of the 'dominant notions of masculinity' in some schools is the avoidance of school work (*ibid.*). Indeed, being an achieving boy has been found to be the key marker in singling out a boy for bullying and homophobic abuse.

It seems that feminised boys come in for a major portion of abuse in both primary and secondary schools, and this abuse is conflated with both misogyny and homophobia. In the primary school context, the worst thing a boy can be called is a 'girl', even worse than being called 'gay boy', 'poof' or 'sissy' . . . and it is certainly feminised to be seen to work in most schools, both primary and secondary.

(Epstein *et al.* 1988: 103)

Thus the rejection of 'feminine' school work is simultaneously a defence against being teased and bullied as gay.

Task 7

In a playgroup one boy was overheard saying to another boy, 'Why do you just sit reading? Girls read, boys play football!' (Siraj-Blatchford and Clarke 2000: 8).

What are the issues involved here? How would you attempt to break down such gender stereotypes?

Encouraging boys to talk about difference

MacNaughton in Skelton (2001: 176) suggests that instead of teachers imposing their models of what boys should be like, they should engage with boys in dialogue along the following lines:

- Talking with boys about which masculinities they find desirable and why this is so.
- Exploring with them the difficulties involved in different ways of being masculine.
- Exposing the occasions when boys make choices about how to be boys and the knock-on effects of those choices.
- Curtailing those boys who are violent and aggressive and offering strong support to those who are non-violent.
- Providing different images of masculinity and help them to develop definitions of masculinity that redefine what it means to be brave, strong, admirable and so on.

However, not all boys are doing badly at school and not all girls are successful at school. The key variables of class and ethnicity are critical in contextualising 'boys' academic failure' and are discussed in the next section.

A discussion of how the variables of gender, class and 'race' operate together

It is important to remember that all learners, whether boys or girls, have a complex identity. Learners' complex identities are based upon many changing variables, some of which may be related to class, geographical location, age, sexuality, gender, ethnicity, language, ability/disability and relationships. Hence, being a boy or a girl is just a part, albeit a very important part, of a learner's complex and shifting identity. Boys (and girls) should not be lumped together as if boys are failures and girls are successful. It is critical to hold on to the understanding that while there are many boys who are not performing well at school, there are many others who are doing very well indeed. Equally, while many girls are performing well at school many other girls do not achieve. There is tremendous diversity within the generalised categories of boy and girl and no hard and fast rules apply.

Gillborn and Mirza (2000) examined the relative importance of the three best-known dimensions of inequality: gender, class and 'race'. In 1997 the gap between boys and girls attaining five or more A*– C grade passes at GCSE was ten percentage points; the gap between African-Caribbean children and white children was eighteen percentage points and the difference between the middle and working class was a staggering fifty percentage points! Hence, in contrast to the disproportionate media attention, Ofsted data shows gender to be a less problematic issue than the significant disadvantage of 'race' and the even greater inequality of class. When academic performance is put into context within the variables of class and 'race', the significance of gender is greatly diminished. As we have seen, this does not deny that there are significant differences between the genders but rather that the issue of class is considerably more important in terms of academic attainment. The relationship between class and academic performance is so close that an analysis of a child's parental class and the parents' levels of education can sometimes be reliably used to predicate a child's success in school examinations. The relationship between class and academic performance can clearly be seen by examining the 'league table' of school examination results throughout the UK. The poorest and most deprived local education authorities are consistently positioned lowest in the league tables and the wealthiest, most middle-class local education authorities, are invariably found at the top!

An analysis of Ofsted's research shows that working-class African-Caribbean boys are disproportionately disadvantaged and may be more vulnerable to exclusionary pressures and poor academic achievement. This is a generalisation and does not mean that all African-Caribbean boys are doing equally badly at school. Indeed, middle-class African-Caribbean boys are generally successful at school. Schools need to be aware that certain groups of students are at risk of exclusionary pressures and poor academic performance and schools need to take the necessary structural and cultural action to avoid failure. However, it is important to note that there are working-class boys who are caring and academically successful and African-Caribbean boys who are capable, well behaved and academically successful. Equally, we might find middle-class girls who are underachieving. This should not surprise us, but rather confirm the complexity of individual identities and circumstances.

Summary and key points

This chapter has defined the key terms of sex, gender and gender stereotyping. The main issues involved in the Nature/Nurture debate have been critically analysed and the historical ways in which the male and female genders have been socially constructed in opposition to each other has been examined. We have reflected upon the complex ways in which children 'police and patrol' their own stereotypical gender roles. We have discussed the 'gender gap' at public examinations in historical and contemporary times and how issues of class and 'race' are more significant than gender in predicting pupils' attainments. Specifically, the chapter has shown how boys and girls cannot be generalised about and that gender is but one aspect of a learner's identity. In particular we have examined the ways in which the construction of masculinity and femininity contributes to some boys' poor performance at school.

Questions to aid reflection

1 Did your family have gendered attitudes and expectations for you or your siblings?
2 How did your local community, culture, religion and nationality affect your family's attitudes to gender?
3 How do the gender issues raised in this chapter manifest themselves within your workplace environment?

Annotated bibliography

Epstein, D., Elwood, J., Hey, V. and Maw, J. (eds) (1999) *Failing Boys? Issues in Gender and Achievement,* Buckingham: Open University Press.
This wide-ranging book examines the current emphasis on boys.
Frater, G. (2000) *Securing Boys' Literacy: A Survey of Effective Practice in Primary Schools*, London: The Basic Skills Agency.
This booklet gives an overview of some practical whole-school tasks that may encourage boys to succeed in literacy.
MacNaughton, G. (2000) *Rethinking Gender in Early Childhood*, London: Paul Chapman Publishing.
This is an excellent book for understanding more about the theory and practice of how children learn their genders in the early years.

Skelton, C. (2001) *Schooling the Boys: Masculinities and Primary Education,*
Buckingham: Open University Press.

A fascinating book providing in-depth analysis of the ways in which boys'
and male teachers' masculinities are constructed within a primary school.

Website

www.bstubbs.co.uk

This website clearly outlines girls' and boys' academic attainments at GCSE
and 'A'-level.

Bibliography

Arnot, M., David, M. and Weiner, G. (1999) *Closing the Gender Gap: Postwar
Education and Social Change*, Oxford: Polity Press.

Cameron, C., Moss, P. and Owen, C. (1999) *Men in the Nursery: Gender and
Caring Work*, London: Paul Chapman Publishing.

Channel 4 (2001) *A Child's World: Boys and Girls*, Programme 3, 29 September.

Cohen M. (1998) 'A habit of healthy idleness: boys' underachievement in
historical perspective', in Epstein, D., Elwood, J., Hey, V. and Maw, J. (eds)
Failing Boys? Issues in Gender and Achievement, Buckingham: Open
University Press.

Epstein, D., Elwood, J., Hey, V. and Maw, J. (1998) *Failing Boys? Issues in
Gender and Achievement*, Buckingham: Open University Press.

Gillborn, D. and Mirza, H. (2000) *Educational Inequality; Mapping Race, Class
and Gender: A Synthesis of Research Evidence*, London: Ofsted.

Jackson, in Epstein, D., Elwood, J., Hey, V. and Maw, J. (1998) *Failing Boys?
Issues in Gender and Achievement*, Buckingham: Open University Press.

Lloyd, B. (1987) 'Social representations of gender', in J. Bruner and H. Haste
(eds) *Making Sense: The Child's Construction of the World*, London:
Routledge.

Mac an Ghaill, M. (1994) *The Making of Men: Masculinities, Sexualities and
Schooling*, Buckingham: Open University Press.

Paetcher, C. (1998) *Educating the Other: Gender, Power and Schooling,*
London: Falmer Press.

Siraj-Blatchford, I. and Clarke, P. (2000) *Supporting Identity, Diversity and
Language in the Early Years*, Buckingham: Open University Press.

Skelton, C. (2001) *Schooling the Boys: Masculinities and Primary Education,*
Buckingham: Open University Press.

MacNaughton, G. (2000) *Rethinking Gender in Early Childhood,* London: Paul
Chapman Publishing.

Walkerdine, V. (1990) *Schoolgirl Fictions*, London: Verso.

Citizenship

Lynn Revell

Introduction

The aim of this chapter is to introduce readers to the discussions surrounding the induction of Citizenship Education into schools and to outline what this will mean for many schools.

By the end of this chapter you should have:

- considered why the Labour government has supported the introduction of Citizenship Education into schools;
- considered the type of citizen that teachers and schools are expected to promote through Citizenship Education;
- understood the breakdown of the three elements of Citizenship Education and their possible implications for schools.

Citizenship Education is meant to take up only 5 per cent of the curriculum but its objectives and influence can be felt throughout the government's reforms in education. The ethos placed at the beginning of the new National Curriculum and the statement of core values placed at the end of the curriculum indicate a new emphasis on the promotion of values and citizenship in schools. All schools can expect to play a significantly new role in the education of children for citizenship in the immediate future.

Citizenship Education – then and now

Other countries have long traditions of teaching children about citizenship but in this country we have tended to stress the importance of the past, empire and tradition. In America at least 40 states require by law some form of political education in high schools but in England a knowledge of the workings of government are merely assumed.

Previous attempts to introduce citizenship in schools were usually ignored. The National Curriculum Council (NCC) identified five cross-curricular themes in 1989: (1) Education for Citizenship; (2) Economic and Industrial Understanding; (3) Health Education; (4) Careers Education and Guidance; and (5) Environmental Education. The NCC stated that they were not 'subjects as such' but should be addressed through other subjects and 'enriched and reinforced by being woven into the wider work of the school in the community' (NCC 8 1990).

Although citizenship was introduced as a cross-curricular theme in the National Curriculum, in effect it disappeared without a trace from most English schools. As a cross-curricular theme, citizenship often appeared irrelevant or simply unhelpful (Rowe and Newton 1994: 16). Research on the recommended cross-curricular themes showed that not only was citizenship a neglected subject in schools but also of all the cross-curricular themes, it was the one that teachers were least likely to focus on. Teachers assumed it was an underlying theme that did not need any explicit teaching or highlighting and that therefore it was ignored as a distinct subject.

Task 1

Speak to as many teachers as possible. Ask them whether they think it is more appropriate for citizenship to be taught explicitly, or whether it should be done through other subjects.

The current context

Why is it that the Labour government has succeeded in prioritising Citizenship Education when other initiatives have either faded away or died due to lack of systematic political and educational support?

The most commonly given reason for the introduction of Citizenship Education is the perceived belief that there is a combined crisis of values and democracy in England. Voter apathy, especially among the young, and the loss of respect for major institutions, like the monarchy and parliament, are often cited as evidence of a decline in values and support for society. Almost everyone agrees that there is a crisis and that education has a key role to play in its alleviation.

The sense of political decline and loss is evident in the report of the Citizen Advisory Group (1998), established by the government to look at citizenship in schools, the Crick Report, as well as in the reports of other government bodies. These twin crises are frequently cited as the justification for Citizenship Education and the reason that it has been brought into being. Just as politicians cite the fall in voting among young people, their disengagement from society and key institutions and the rise in criminal behaviour as the reason for promoting Citizenship Education, it is also claimed that Citizenship Education is the first step towards countering these problems.

There appears to be a consensus that there is a general crisis of values in Western society, and particularly among children and young people. From the church, to information provided by polls, the evidence seems to confirm the view that young people are disengaged from society.

In 1997 the Archbishop of Canterbury launched a 'moral crusade in the nation's classrooms'. He believed that the absence of a common core of articulated values and the growth of individualism had undermined traditional morality and that the ensuing crisis was most acute among the young.

Other polls have found that in the last General Election only 57 per cent of people between the ages of 17–25 voted and 67 per cent said that they felt they had no obligation towards society. One-third of 18–34-year-olds see themselves as outside the system and less than one-sixth thought they had a duty to vote (Potter 1999).

These findings were confirmed by a report carried out and funded by the Prince's Trust, and the Commission on Citizenship on young people's views on democracy, community and citizenship. The research found that young people were mostly divorced from communities and did not feel a part of society. Although the young people involved came from a variety of backgrounds, the authors claim there was one over-riding theme in their data that united all the interviewees. The common theme was 'a strong call for more teaching of the issues surrounding "citizenship" in schools (Richardson 1990: 35).

In response to a desire to establish a common core of values that could be introduced through education, the government itself initiated an attempt to discover these values. In 1996 the School Curriculum and Assessment Authority (SCAA) established the National Forum for Values in Education, the express aim of which was to negotiate the possible existence of a set of common core values that could be promoted in schools. The forum's brief was to discover moral values that were not only non-negotiable, but which schools could endorse and transmit (Beck 1998: 86).

The second reason that is often given for the need for Citizenship Education, and one which forms a crucial backdrop to the whole debate, is the perceived failure of previous forms of education to inculcate morality into the young. In England moral education has traditionally been channelled through religion in schools. The White Paper preceding the 1944 Education Act called upon schools and Religious Education to 'revive the personal and spiritual values of the nation' (Board of Education 1943, quoted in Cox and Cairns 1989: 10).

This faith in Religious Education could not be sustained as Christianity played an ever-decreasing role in the life of the nation. As recently as the 1950s, as church attendance declined, the institutions of the family and the monarchy and the establishment were no longer as respected or valued as they once were. It was clear that Religious Education as the conveyer of moral education was no longer relevant (*ibid.*: 14). The majority not only chose to absent themselves from church (except to be married or buried) but also, as we moved into the new millennium, there was a greater interest in the exotic alternatives provided by the new age than in traditional Christianity.

The place of Religious Education as defined by the 1988 Education Act confirmed the diminished status of mainstream religion in England. Many Church of England leaders were dismayed at the 'totally inadequate treatment of RE on the consultative paper on the National Curriculum' (*Church Times* 2 October 1987) and they had to fight to ensure that Religious Education was considered a foundation subject.

The architects of Citizenship Education believe that the combined efforts of moral and spiritual education and Religious Education have failed to encourage sufficient moral awareness in children. Religious Education and attempts to create a meaningful role for it in the curriculum are seen to have failed (Hargreaves 1994: 34). It is partly the failure of the existing mechanisms to encourage moral sensibility into school children that warrants the introduction of a new kind of moral education, namely, Citizenship Education.

The moral crisis among the young, the failure of Religious Education and the political disengagement of key sectors of the population provide the context in which Citizenship Education has emerged as a radical addition to English education. These factors explain why Citizenship Education has gained so much support at this time. However, as we shall see in the next section, these factors also explain why Citizenship Education, as promoted by the Labour government, takes the form it does.

Task 2

Can you find evidence of the values your school promotes through documentation and written reports? You could also find evidence of your school ethos in home/school contracts, the topic chosen for assemblies, the approach to discipline, and classroom and playground rules. If your school has a mission statement, look at the statement and try to work out a list of values you think your school supports.

Once you have worked out the values you think your school supports, look at the Statement of Values by the National Forum for Values in Education and Community at the back of the National Curriculum. Are there any similarities between these values and the ones promoted by your school?

Active citizenship

In his book on moral development in schools John Beck tells the story of a head teacher who addressed an audience of 400 postgraduate Certificate of Education students, commenting that he would be happy to deal with Citizenship Education 'as soon as someone tells us what education for citizenship is' (Beck 1998: 96). That same head teacher today would find that the government has more than satisfied his plea for an explanation of Citizenship Education. In a number of key documents such as *Learning to be a Citizen, Encouraging Citizenship* or the Crick Report, the requirements, as they are laid down in the National Curriculum, provide a clear picture of what the government wants Citizenship Education to be.

The type of citizenship education that is celebrated in the Crick Report, which secondary teachers are mandated to teach and which primary teachers will be inspected on, is a very specific type of citizenship. Citizenship, as understood by Crick, is not an entitlement but primarily a responsibility of the individual, and is normally referred to as 'active citizenship'. It is the active citizen that stands at the centre of the government's proposals on citizenship and it is the active citizen that teachers are encouraged to cultivate, promote and reward in the classroom. Although Citizenship Education is divided into different areas and its character changes from Key Stage to Key Stage and from subject to subject, it is the celebration and cultivation of the active citizen that unite all the different strands.

In 1988 a Commission was established to investigate citizenship under the auspices of the House of Commons. In the opening paragraphs of its report *Encouraging Citizenship*, it states that its aim was 'to consider how best to encourage, develop and recognize Active Citizenship within a wide range of groups in the community, both local and national, including school students and adults' (Commission for Citizenship 1990: 1).

In the Crick Report active citizenship is defined as a form of citizenship that is comprised of rights and duties. That is, individuals, as citizens, have as many obligations to the nation as they can expect rights. There are no rights without responsibilities (Citizenship Advisory Group 1998: 10). Active citizens are not just people who expect society to protect their rights, active citizens are involved in society and carry out their responsibilities. Active citizenship is not merely the physical activity of the individual but is composed of three elements: the social, civil/community and the political. An outline of the content of each element, as recommended by the Crick Report and the National Curriculum for Key Stages 1 and 2, shows not only how important the idea of active citizenship is to modern citizenship education, but also the role the government expects teachers and schools to play in the creation of young citizens.

Social and moral responsibility

Although the strands take equal place within the curriculum, according to the Crick Report, social and moral responsibility is 'near the heart of the matter' (Citizenship Advisory Group 1998: 11). Education in social and moral responsibility is about pupils learning appropriate attitudes and behaviour of themselves and towards others. Its aim is to encourage children to adopt certain attitudes and responses to authority, social responsibility, the law and decision-making. Active citizenship demands a disposition towards democratic behaviour and practice and the task of the Social and Moral Responsibility strand of Citizenship Education is to facilitate that understanding and disposition.

The Crick Report rebuts the idea that primary school education is in any way pre-political or pre-citizenship and it stresses the need for primary age children to learn about social and moral responsibility from the very beginning (*ibid.*: 11). It argues that children are never too young to learn about the appropriate ways of conducting themselves, managing their feelings or their relationships with others.

In the National Curriculum for primary schools this aspect of active citizenship is evident in all the sections: Developing confidence and responsibility and making the most of their abilities, and the sections on Preparing to play an active role as citizens, Developing a healthy, safer lifestyle and Developing good relationships and respecting the difference between people. At Key Stage 2 pupils will be expected to be able to respond to issues like racism, recognise the significance of help-lines and be able to reflect on moral, spiritual and cultural issues.

The inclusion of moral and spiritual issues in education is not new. The 1995 SCAA working paper on moral and spiritual development outlined key moral values for schools to promote with children. The *SCAA Discussion Paper on Spiritual and Moral Development* even went so far as to list the values that schools should include and reject and suggests that there are absolute values which teachers should introduce to young children.

There are areas of similarity between the moral education as it is presented by SCAA and its new incarnation in Citizenship Education. Both versions are committed to moral absolutes that they list and both stress that understanding and knowledge are essential strands in the process of moral education. Where they differ is in the outcomes they expect pupils to demonstrate. The SCAA document lists the values it thinks children should learn at school, but two paragraphs later it acknowledges that 'Society permits, even if it does not promote, a range of behaviour which is considered wrong by some, often many, of its members' (SCAA 1995: 6). It goes on to insist that pupils have 'to make up their own minds on these and other issues' and then argues that ultimately the task of moral education is to give pupils the skills and reasoning abilities through which they can make up their minds.

> The task of schools, in partnership with the home, is to furnish pupils with the knowledge and the ability to question and reason which will enable them to develop their own value system and to make responsible decisions on such matters.
>
> *(ibid.* 6)

SCAA's belief that the task of schools is to facilitate children's abilities to make their own moral decisions has more in common with the ethos of the values clarification system of moral education than with the model presented within Citizenship Education. In the framework established by values clarification, teachers aimed not to instil a preconceived set of moral codes into their pupils but to encourage them to develop their own morals. The objective was the process of providing the contexts and the time for pupils to develop their reasoning skills.

Similarly, the SCAA document lists a number of outcomes it expects the morally educated school leaver should understand. Of the eight outcomes, six deal with aspects of understanding morality and only two of them deal with actions or behaviour and one of these concerns the ability of pupils to behave in accordance with their own principles rather than those outlined by SCAA itself (*ibid.*: 6).

The model of moral education proposed in the Crick Report and Citizenship Education, as outlined in the National Curriculum, has an entirely different rationale. Moral responsibility as described in the National Curriculum is not just the inclusion of ideas and values that once found their home in a

SCAA document. The SCAA document referred to moral development, but the Crick Report and the National Curriculum both talk about developing moral responsibility.

The difference between moral development and moral responsibility is clearly illustrated in the context of active citizenship. Moral education, as defined as a part of active citizenship, is not merely teaching children to understand and value certain morals. It encourages children to act according to their moral principles. The 1995 SCAA document recognised that pupils have the will and the ability to act morally but the emphasis is on their understanding and their ability to rationalise their moral ideas. In contrast, under Citizenship Education pupils are expected to demonstrate their understanding and awareness of issues by acting them out.

The concluding section at the end of Key Stage 1 and 2 is breadth of opportunities where the National Curriculum states that during their lessons 'pupils should be taught the *knowledge, skills and understanding* through opportunities to . . . ' (DfEE 1999: 138). The National Curriculum lists a range of options that teachers can use to encourage pupils to demonstrate practically their awareness and understanding of the issues covered in the subject.

The emphasis on expecting pupils to demonstrate their ability to behave appropriately is reflected in other sections of the National Curriculum on Citizenship Education. At Key Stage 1 pupils should be able to recognise their feelings but also to know that their actions have consequences for others and for themselves. Pupils at Key Stage 1 should be encouraged to talk about these ideas but teachers must also teach pupils the relevant skills to be able to act out these requirements. Similarly, at Key Stage 2, pupils should not only be able to discuss a variety of moral and social issues but the National Curriculum states that they could be given suitable responsibilities and duties as a way of developing skills in these areas.

Community involvement

Many schools have links with their community. Pupils help with fund-raising and celebrate festivals within the community. Most schools have a relationship with the fire and police services and increasingly schools are making links with companies and firms that can offer them resources in the form of sponsorship for sports or IT equipment.

The idea of the community more generally underlies the government's definition of the active citizen. Active citizens are active not as random individuals who pursue their objectives, but as members of a shared community. In her book on the place of virtues in education Patricia White (1996) argues that a coherent society needs shared hopes or social hopes that relate to everyone in that community. The existence of shared hopes as they are experienced in communities is essential to the activities of individuals as citizens.

Community involvement as it is imagined within Citizenship Education institutionalises the concept of community involvement in the life of all schools. Where community involvement was once the choice of individual schools, it is now a practical requirement for all schools teaching Citizenship Education.

The reason for community involvement in Citizenship Education is twofold. The first is that the emphasis on moral and social responsibility necessitates that pupils are able to demonstrate their understanding in some practical manner. A curriculum that suggests that pupils engage with voluntary helpers, are familiar with the purpose of help-lines and 'learn to take part more fully in school and community activities' (DfEE 1999: 139) assumes that schools already have some sort of relationship with their communities. Schools which do not have a relationship with their communities would find it difficult to provide the opportunities demanded by the National Curriculum for their pupils to demonstrate their awareness and understanding of the issues underlying Citizenship Education.

The expectation that community involvement will become a part of school life is integral to the idea of the active citizen itself. Active citizens, envisioned by the Crick Report and in the National Curriculum, are citizens that not only understand their rights but also are predisposed to involve themselves in the running and organization of their community. In this sense, community involvement at school is preparation for the involvement the government would like to see them carry out as adult citizens.

The second reason for the inclusion of community involvement as a prescribed strand within Citizenship Education is the government's belief that the actual experience of real participation is essential to the process of creating 'a democratic disposition' (White 1996: 1) or a commitment to citizenship in pupils. Pupils who participate when they are young will be more likely to participate as adults because their childhood experiences will have transformed their understanding of themselves and their relationship to society in a way that traditional lessons cannot do.

The belief that actual participation reinforces and structures learning for citizenship is evident across all the Key Stages, but some writers suggest that this is particularly true for children at primary school. *You, Me, Us!* is an extensive scheme of work published by the Citizenship Foundation and sponsored by the Home Office. It is specifically designed for primary schools and aims to aid teachers and schools promote social and moral responsibility. In a section on Community Building, the authors note that, in relation to taking others into account, the process is generally intellectual and emotional, but for young children the element of empathy in the context of involvement is essential for the development of these sentiments (Rowe and Newton 1994: 15). Similarly the Local Government Information Unit believes that when young children are encouraged from a very early age to be involved in decision-making the process helps 'to nurture a confidence in local democratic processes' (Willow 1997: 5).

Ultimately, the age of the pupils involved will determine the nature of their community involvement but, however young they are, schools need to be aware that they will be expected to provide opportunities and forums where even the very youngest child can participate.

Task 3

Read the guidelines for Citizenship Education in the Key Stage you are most familiar with. How many of the recommendations are suited to community involvement?

If your school has links with the community in what way could those links be adapted so that pupils in your school could fulfil the requirements for community involvement set out in the National Curriculum?

Political literacy

The Crick Report stresses that political literacy is more than mere knowledge of the workings of government and democracy. Political literacy is meant to encompass knowledge and awareness of the whole spectrum of political activity from the personal world of employment and taxation to the procedures surrounding international conflict resolution (Citizenship Advisory Group 1998: 13). The National Curriculum details the areas of knowledge children will be expected to know in this area across all age phases. At Key Stage 1 children's knowledge is restricted to awareness of basic political and social concepts like fairness, right and wrong and the source of money, but Key Stage 2 children will be expected to understand and use specific political language (DfEE 1999: 140).

The government believes that political literacy is important as one of the reasons young people are disengaged from the political process is because of their ignorance of those processes. They hope that educating children in the workings of local, national and international politics will go some way to guaranteeing their future interest and commitment to democratic institutions and practices.

True to its belief that there is no such thing as a pre-political school child, the Crick Report and the National Curriculum expect teachers to introduce basic political knowledge from the time pupils enter school. Although there is some doubt whether children younger than seven can understand political ideas and concepts, the introduction of Citizenship Education means that children at Key Stage 1 will encounter them in some form.

A second reason for the inclusion of political literacy is that the type of citizenship promoted within Citizenship Education is characterised by an emphasis on obtaining and exercising democratic skills. Active citizenship demands that individuals know something of political definitions and that they are also competent and capable of using that knowledge. It is a form of citizenship that assumes individuals have certain skills. Political literacy in the context of active citizenship, and outlined in the Crick Report, is a combination of the skills, knowledge, aptitudes and skills necessary for an individual to operate in a democratic society: 'We stress, however, that citizenship education is education for citizenship, behaving and acting as a citizen, therefore it is not just knowledge of citizenship and civil society; it also implies developing values, skills and understanding' (Citizenship Advisory Group 1998: 13).

Task 4

Look through your school's schemes of work for one curriculum subject other than Citizenship Education. What opportunities (if any) can you detect for political literacy within that subject?

Summary and key points

Citizenship Education has been a long time coming. While other democracies have assumed that educational programmes on citizenship are a part of the democratic tradition itself, this country is about to introduce a model in order to counter the perceived breakdown of democracy. The discussions surrounding the background to the establishment of Citizenship Education, the creation of the National Forum for Values and recent research into the views and political habits of the young have all centred around the idea that it will counter the perceived crisis of values and democracy in society.

There is an ongoing discussion about the meaning of citizenship but from the very beginning of the project to introduce Citizenship Education in this country, the idea of Active Citizenship has dominated the educational agenda. Active citizens are expected to be proactive and sympathetic towards democracy and existing institutions within society, they will be predisposed towards the democratic process and already experienced in community involvement by the time they leave school.

This chapter has provided some of the background to the emergence of Citizenship Education and highlighted some of the expectations as they are described in the most recent publications. Citizenship as an idea, let alone Citizenship Education, is an area where there are vast differences of interpretation between academics, educators and politicians.

Educators in schools and student teachers often say that in good schools, good educators are already carrying out many of the demands of Citizenship Education. Many schools are involved in projects, ways of teaching and initiatives that are well ahead of some of the suggested activities in the National Curriculum and which are adventurous and educationally innovative. Nevertheless, the sum total of Citizenship Education does represent something unique in British education and this change will bring far reaching and possibly unexpected consequences and demands on pupils and schools.

Questions to aid reflection

1 How realistic are the aims and objectives of Citizenship Education as they are described in the National Curriculum?
2 Do you think that Citizenship Education will remain a part of British education or that it is a 'fad' that will pass away?
3 If you were in charge of Citizenship Education in your school, how would you support other teachers in their attempts to introduce it as a new subject?

Annotated bibliography

Beck, J. (1998) *Morality and Citizenship in Education*, London: Cassell.
   Provides a thorough and detailed background of the place of citizenship and values education in British schools.
Citizenship Advisory Group (1998) *Education for Citizenship and the Teaching of Democracy in Schools* (the Crick Report), London: QCA.
   An important booklet for all those who want to understand the government's rationale for introducing Citizenship Education into schools.
Rowe, D. and Newton, J. (eds) (1994) *You, Me, Us!* London: Citizenship Foundation.
   A good example of the type of work used in schools to teach Citizenship Education.

Bibliography

Beck, J. (1998) *Morality and Citizenship in Education*, London: Cassell.
Citizenship Advisory Group. (1998) *Education for Citizenship and the Teaching of Democracy in Schools* (the Crick Report), London: QCA.

Commission for Citizenship (1988) *Encouraging Citizenship*, London: HMSO.

Cox, E. and Cairns, J. (1989) *Problems and Possibilities for Religious Education,* London: Hodder and Stoughton.

DfEE (1999) *The National Curriculum*, London: HMSO.

Hargreaves, D. (1994) *The Mosaic of Learning: Schools and Teachers for the Next Century*, London: Demos.

National Curriculum Council (1990) *Curriculum Guidance 8: Education for Citizenship*, York: NCC.

Potter, J. (1999) *Education for Life, Work and Citizenship*, London: Community Service Volunteer.

Richardson, A. (1990) *Talking About Commitment: The Views of Young People on Citizenship and Volunteering*, London: The Prince's Trust.

Rowe, D. and Newton, J. (eds) (1994) *You, Me, Us!*, London: Citizenship Foundation.

SCAA (1995) *SCAA Discussion Paper on Spiritual and Moral Development*, London: SCAA.

White, P. (1996) *Civic Virtues and Public Schooling*, London: Teacher's College Press.

Willow, C. (1997) *Hear! Hear! Promoting Children and Young People's Democratic Participation in Local Government*, London: Local Government Information Unit.

Index

An 'f' after a page number indicates inclusion of a figure; a 't' indicates inclusion of a table.